Lessons

AVERY

an imprint of Penguin Random House

New York

Lessons

– MY PATH TO A MEANINGFUL LIFE –

Gisele Bündchen

AVERY

an imprint of Penguin Random House LLC
375 Hudson Street
New York, New York 10014

Text copyright © 2018 by Gisele Inc.
Photo on page 1 © Tarciso Lima; photo on page 2 © Paulo Guerra;
photo on page 25 © Vavá Ribeiro; photo on page 92 © Yoshioka/ihateflash;
photo on page 139 © firstVIEW; photo on page 152 © Wesley Santos;
photos on pages 161, 225, and 228 © Nino Mūnoz;
photo on page 194 © Lalo de Almeida.

Most Avery books are available at special quantity discounts for bulk purchase for sales promotions, premiums, fund-raising, and educational needs. Special books or book excerpts also can be created to fit specific needs. For details, write SpecialMarkets@penguinrandomhouse.com.

ISBN 9780525538646
ebook ISBN 9780525538714

Printed in the United States of America
1   3   5   7   9   10   8   6   4   2

Book design by Laura K. Corless

Neither the publisher nor the author is engaged in rendering professional advice or services to the individual reader. The ideas, procedures, and suggestions contained in this book are not intended as a substitute for consulting with your physician. All matters regarding your health require medical supervision. Neither the author nor the publisher shall be liable or responsible for any loss or damage allegedly arising from any information or suggestion in this book.

Penguin is committed to publishing works of quality and integrity. In that spirit, we are proud to offer this book to our readers; however, the story, the experiences, and the words are the author's alone.

To Vivi, Benny and Jack

Thank you for your love, for being the light of my life, for being the most incredible teachers, and allowing me to travel on new roads, discovering deeper meanings and purpose. You are my inspiration every day to do all I can to make the world a better place. *Amo vocês.*

CONTENTS

INTRODUCTION
1

1   It All Starts with Discipline
17

2   Challenges Are Opportunities in Disguise
49

3   The Quality of Your Life Depends on the Quality of Your
     Relationships
75

4   Our Thoughts and Words Are Powerful—Use Them Wisely
107

5   Where Your Attention Goes Is What Grows
133

6   Nature: Our Greatest Teacher
157

7   Take Care of Your Body So It Can Take Care of You
    179

8   Know Thyself
    203

    ACKNOWLEDGMENTS
    231

INTRODUCTION

This photo was taken for my first modeling book when I was fourteen years old.

If my intention was to write a straightforward chronicle of my life so far, the fast-cut version might go like this:

My name is Gisele Caroline Bündchen. I've worked as a fashion model for the past twenty-three years. I was born in 1980 and grew up in Horizontina, a small town in southern Brazil, an hour from where you cross the river to enter Argentina. I'm fifth-generation Brazilian of

German descent on both sides. My parents spoke German with each other and Portuguese to my five sisters and me. I am a middle child, and as kids, my twin sister, Pati, and I used to argue about which one of us was the third or the fourth in age. When I was growing up, I wanted to be either a professional volleyball player or a veterinarian.

When I was thirteen years old, my mom, who worried about my bad posture—I was already 5 feet, 9 inches tall—enrolled two of my sisters and me in a local modeling course. At the end of the course we got to go on a special trip to Curitiba, São Paulo, and Rio de Janeiro. The bus ride there felt endless, twenty-seven hours long. Some of the mothers came with us, including mine. At a São Paulo mall, a man came up to me with a classic creepy-guy line: *Do you want to be a model?* "Mom!" I yelled, and over she ran. But he—Zeca was his name—was for real, a scout for the Elite Model Management. When we went to his offices, he told my mom she should enroll me in a national contest, Elite Look of the Year, and so she did. I couldn't believe it when I won second place, which came with a round-trip plane ticket to Ibiza, Spain, so I could model in the Elite Model Look world contest. It was my first time on a plane, my first trip outside Brazil. Somehow I ended up as one of the ten finalists. Everything was happening fast, fast.

A year later, in 1995, I moved to São Paulo to launch my modeling career. I was fourteen. As you can imagine, moving from a small town of only 17,000 people to the largest city in Brazil was a

Me during the finals for the Elite Model Look contest in São Paulo, 1994. I was fourteen.

An early behind-the-scenes shot from when I was sixteen and shooting in Rio de Janeiro.

big change. After I spent a few months working in São Paulo, the agency sent me to Tokyo, Japan, where I lived for three months doing catalog work. My first big break came a few years later in London, when the designer Alexander McQueen selected me to model in his ready-to-wear show. I went down the runway without a shirt, petrified, a white top painted on at the last minute by a makeup artist, as artificial rain poured down from the ceiling. After the Alexander

McQueen show, the industry gave me a nickname—"The Body"—which stuck.

In 1999, I modeled for Versace, Ralph Lauren, Chloé, Missoni, Valentino, Armani, and Dolce & Gabbana. *Vogue* magazine chose me to represent the end of the "heroin chic" era of modeling. That year I was on the cover of French *Vogue* and three times on the cover of American *Vogue*. The headline on one feature story was "The Return of the Curve." I ended that year winning *Vogue's* Model of the Year Award. In spring 2000, I modeled for Marc Jacobs, Donna Karan, Calvin Klein, Christian Dior, Prada, Valentino, and many other well-known brands in New York, Milan, and Paris. From 1998 to 2003, I appeared in every one of Dolce & Gabbana's fashion campaigns, and from 2000 to 2007, I was one of the Victoria's Secret Angels. In the past twenty years I've appeared on 1,200 magazine covers, 450 fashion editorials, and walked in nearly 500 fashion shows. I deliberately took a step back from modeling in 2015, as I wanted to focus more on my family and personal projects. The last time I walked on a runway was during the opening of the 2016 Summer Olympics in Rio. I came down the longest runway I've ever been on while a pianist played Tom Jobim's "The Girl from Ipanema." It was electrifying! It felt like the culmination of everything that had gone before.

———

Everything above happened—though I've left out all the details. It's the story of the public me. But the life I've lived in public has very little connection to who I really am, or what matters most to me, or what I believe in and want to give back to the world. The irony is that though I'm known for my work as a model, I've never felt that the person on the runway or in magazines and TV commercials was me. In school in Brazil I'd been mocked by my classmates for my height and my weight and my appearance. I don't believe any level of success as an adult completely changes how you saw yourself as a child.

So when I began modeling, even though I supposedly had a model's physique, I felt awkward. It didn't help my confidence when some people in the business told me that my eyes were too small and my nose and boobs were too big. At age fourteen, nothing felt more unsettling or made me feel more self-conscious than a designer telling me I was pretty, or a photographer telling me how to stand, or an editor commenting on my body or my breasts or my eyes or my nose as if I weren't even in the room.

That's why, starting around the age of eighteen, in an effort to protect myself and to avoid getting hurt or feeling objectified, I created a shield around myself. The private me was Gisele, but the model Gisele was *her*. That's what I called her, too—*her*. *She* was an actress. A performer. A chameleon. A made-up character expressing the fantasy of a designer. I showed up at the job. I learned what the photographer wanted, what the stylist wanted, what the makeup artist wanted. Their ideas came together to create a mood, and suddenly I could see *her*, feel *her*. Modeling was a way for me to explore all the colors of my personality, including ones I didn't know I had. As *she* or *her*, I could act out any emotion, any attitude. It was as if by detaching myself I could be free, while keeping the real me hidden and safe. *She* could be sexy or demure. *She* could be a soldier or a brazen woman. *She* could be a face or a body somewhere in between. Modeling had never been my dream—growing up I didn't even know it was an actual profession. I simply saw what was happening to me as an opportunity to make a living. Doors opened—first one, then another—and I walked through them. There was a practical component to it as well. As a child, I had heard my parents arguing about money. I thought if I tried out modeling, and maybe even got good at it, I might be able to help our family, instead of being just one more mouth to feed. So I decided to take the opportunity I was being offered and see what might become of it.

But instead of writing about *her*, I want to focus on who *I* am. So in this book I've laid out the lessons that have helped me live a more conscious and joyful life, inspired me to overcome challenges I've faced over the years (including panic attacks), and given me a deeper understanding of myself and the world around me.

Some of these lessons I learned the hard way—through personal experience. Others I learned through watching others over the years and concluding what *not* to do and how *not* to act. Each of the chapters in this book has stories taken from my own experiences, illustrating my learning process and what was happening in my life at the time. I've had many teachers along the way, too. I've discovered that nature is the most powerful teacher and healer. I've learned to pay attention to my inner voice, which has given me many important insights even when I didn't want to listen. I've learned that our thoughts, words, and actions are all connected, and why we need to be careful with them. I began nourishing my body, mind, and spirit through meditation, healing foods, and a positive outlook, and as a result was able to experience a deeper clarity and greater sense of purpose. I hope that sharing my own story can serve as an inspiration to others and be of help.

So if the model I talked about earlier was a *her*, who am I?

If there's one word I use to describe myself, it's *simple*. I'm a barefoot-jeans-and-T-shirt kind of girl. My family will tell you the same. I've always been a student of life, always curious, always wanting to know more. Naturally, when I left my hometown to begin modeling, I started to experience the world in new ways. Over the next two decades, I began the process of discovering who I was. As I said, that Gisele is very different from my public self. I was born into a hardworking, middle-class family in a city in south-

Me as a baby at home in Horizontina, 1981.

ern Brazil called Três de Maio. Along with my parents, there were six of us girls: Raque, Fofa, Pati, Gise (that's me), Gabi, and Fafi. My mom worked as a teller at a local bank. My dad was an entrepreneur who worked in real estate, as a sales representative—he had so many different jobs. Forever reading, learning, and creating, he was—and still is—a genuine free spirit. Today he is a motivational speaker and sociologist who works with me on environmental projects.

We were lucky to have many varieties of fruit trees in our backyard—avocados; pitanga, which is a kind of red cherry; peach; guava; papaya; butia or jelly palm; and three different kinds of tangerines (my favorite fruit)—which I would fold into the front of my T-shirt and lug home.

I always loved nature. I felt that the dirt or sand under my feet and the trees and the clouds and the birds and the sunlight were a part of who I was, that *I* was nature. I remember how much I loved visiting my grandmother's farm, where she milked cows, grew most of

My dad and my mom (holding Gabi) and in the middle Raque and Fofa, at Pati's and my birthday party (that's me in the front left, making a face). Brazilian birthday cakes are usually made with condensed milk and are absolutely delicious!

what she ate, and sewed her own clothes. She would cook us delicious food such as *cuca*, a German version of panettone, but with tiny chunks of strawberries or grapes baked into it, which she served with fresh heavy cream still warm from the milk bucket.

I grew up Roman Catholic, and my mom made us go to church every Sunday. Like my sisters, I wasn't all that happy sitting on a hard bench, listening to the priest talking. But I did love the singing (my mom had a loud, beautiful soprano voice) and, afterward, eating whatever dishes the church ladies set out—cabbage salad, pasta, and *churrasco*, a way of grilling meat and chicken on a stick—with the other kids. I still love the stories in the Bible, and I teach them to my own children. But I was always digging and digging to find out the *why* of everything, and at some point I began questioning what I was being taught.

One day in religion class when I was twelve or thirteen years old, we were studying Leviticus. I raised my hand. How could the mandate "an eye for an eye, a tooth for a tooth" exist side by side with Jesus teaching us we should love our enemies and always turn the other cheek? How did *that* work? I wasn't trying to be smart, but it made no sense. Instead of answering the question or starting a discussion, the

Left: My sister Pati's and my birthday party, 1987, Horizontina. I think you can tell how happy I was after waiting a whole year to get Fofura, my favorite doll ever! *Right:* Pati and I loved playing with the chickens at my grandmother's home, 1983. It was my favorite place to go as a child.

teacher looked surprised, and then frustrated, and sent me to the principal. I didn't think I'd done anything wrong! (I still don't.)

Why couldn't she give me an answer? If she couldn't, who would? Not my parents. My mom and dad were too busy running around working while trying to raise six girls. And the questions I wanted answers to were accumulating. Who was I? Why was I here? How did the world begin? As the questions increased, so did my resistance against any kind of system that said, *These are the facts, this is how it works, and there's only one way.*

Maybe it was my constant searching that led me to be fascinated by the world of spirit. I'd pray at night to God, to my star, to my guardian angels. In my early teens I began reading not just about religion but belief and metaphysics and mythology. Those are still my favorite subjects. At some point I began believing that all of us live in a world ruled by illusions, and that my—our—job is to find out who we truly are, and discover our individual purpose. Everything we experience, good and bad, has a meaning, even if we may not understand it right away. It's all happening for us to learn.

I tell my own children that God is an energy that stands behind the creation of everything. God is visible in the mountains, the oceans, the sky, the trees, the sunlight, the rain, the animals, and the seasons. Without nature, nothing and no one would exist. Nature is divine, and is what keeps us all alive.

Today, at age thirty-eight, I feel I'm on the cusp of a whole new life—a rebirth of sorts. My goal now is to continue learning, and developing my talents in order to use whatever gifts I have to help serve the greater good. I believe many people are preoccupied and distracted by information overload and bad news, and my hope is that this book can serve as an inspiration tool that focuses instead on internal, spiritual values. When I was young, I had no way of predicting what would happen to me twenty years later. I was too busy living, too busy making choices. I once read that when we look back on our life, we can see a story line or an order or a plan, as if it were composed by an invisible force—and that the events and even the people in it that seemed random or unimportant at the time become in the end indispensable to our story. Our lives play an important role in the lives of others, too. It's as if our lives were cogs in one great dream of a lone dreamer in which all the characters are also dreaming. When we look back, it's as if, without knowing it, we were all co-creating our lives—but how, though, and with whom?

I know that I'm still relatively young, but looking back on my own life so far, I feel an enormous sense of gratitude. I've been given phenomenal opportunities, and I have worked hard to make the most out of each of them. My life didn't just happen to me. I *chose* to move to São Paulo when I was fourteen. Many years later I *chose* to marry my husband. I *chose* to have our two children. I could have never left Brazil. I could have played professional volleyball (I was good at it) or become a veterinarian. I could have married somebody else, or never married, or never had children. The life I live today is an accumulation of dozens of decisions I have made. When I was younger, I took advantage of the doors that swung open for me. But as I've gotten older, I've started to push the doors open—for myself. If we make choices more consciously, and with greater self-awareness, we will find ourselves more closely aligned to our purpose in life, whatever it may be.

Over the years, friends and strangers have confided in me about the struggles of the girls and women in their lives. They've told me that their daughters or friends were facing depression, anxiety, eating disorders, self-harm—and in response I've shared some of my *own* challenging experiences with the hope that they would feel supported and know they were not alone. We are all bombarded today with images of how we should look, and how we should behave. And yes, I know that for more than two decades I worked in an industry that can have a tendency to exalt unattainable images of beauty, style, and glamour. I know, too, that social media is about showcasing the best moments of our lives, not the worst ones. On my own Instagram, you won't find a lot of photos of me with a headache or with bags under my eyes from staying up all night with my children when they get sick.

Life can be magical. But living it well takes work, focus, patience, compassion, determination, and discipline. Jealousy, or comparing yourself with *anyone*, is a toxic recipe. Jealousy only produces feelings of never being good enough. I believe we are—each of us—singular in our own way. We each have something unique to offer, which only *we* can give to the world.

Many women, I know, are simply overwhelmed. Whether they are in high school with too many activities in their schedules, or in their thirties and forties being run ragged while trying to be a good mom, a perfect wife, a star at work, or all three, they spend almost no time alone. They've lost a connection to nature and to themselves. They're looking for answers outside themselves, not realizing that the answers that matter most are on the *inside*. There was a time when I *was* that person. So naturally I'm also writing this book to my younger self. If someone had shared these lessons with me when I was in my teens and twenties, maybe my own ride would have been a bit easier. And I want to share these lessons with my own children, too. I always ask myself, *In what way could I help them cope if they weren't my children? Or if I weren't here? How can I leave them something valuable and important?* The lessons contained in this book are the ones I most want my own children to learn and remember as guiding lights in their own lives.

For twenty-three years I was a student in the school of fashion, and one of the first things I discovered was how shallow it could be. A lot of the time being a model made me feel torn and guilty. Modeling was never my passion or my identity. It was a work opportunity that appeared when I was very young, and I took it. That isn't to say I'm not extremely grateful for all the opportunities I was given or to the people who offered them. Today, whatever visibility I have is because of my work in fashion, and now I can use some of the tools I've acquired to bring more attention to projects that are closer to my heart and that I believe can have a positive impact in the world. Most people know me only as an image. An object. A blank canvas on which they can project their own stories, or dreams, or fantasies—which, ironically, was the same approach I took at work when I became *she*, and *her*! For twenty-three years, I've also been an image without a voice. I have this in common with lots of women. Haven't most of us gotten the message that our voices aren't worth hearing, whether we're being ignored in a meeting, or criticized online, or reduced to a bunch of body parts? Allowing myself to be open and vulnerable—not *her*, but me, Gisele—is very scary. I won't be able to detach or hide anymore. At the same time, take it from me: nothing feels stranger than to be the object of someone else's projections. To be known but also unknown no longer feels right to me. Life is not always easy, nor is it a fairy tale, and we all go through challenges, no matter who we are. By speaking up, I hope I can inspire other women to do the same, especially at a time when women *need* to support

During the Gauchos Day celebration, Horizontina, September 1986. I was the one in the orange dress.

other women more than ever. After all, changes only come about when we are willing to stand for what we believe.

The lessons in this book are not rules. As someone who has always questioned the status quo, I certainly don't want to become anyone's status quo. Some of these lessons may come across as common sense or familiar. My goal is simply to interpret specific beliefs in the context of my own life and experiences. And like most people, I'm still learning as I go and trying to improve every day. If these lessons are useful, great. If one, two, or all eight of them don't resonate with you, let them go and move on. Remember, I grew up questioning anyone or anything that claimed to have the answer, and you might feel the same way. I'm not pretending to be an authority or an expert even for a second. I'm no better or worse than anyone else. These lessons have simply worked for *me* and helped make my *own* life better by giving it deeper meaning.

Still, if you walk away with just one message from this book, I hope it's the importance of living your life with love. Loving yourself. Loving other people. Loving the world in which we all live. Throw away everything else, but please, please don't ever live your life without love.

1

It All Starts with Discipline

Discipline is a hard word to love, especially when we're young. *Can't I put off thinking about that for a few more years?* It's a word that sounds like it belongs in the military or a boarding school, or on a list of rules and regulations that keep us from doing what we want to do. Discipline can sometimes seem like the enemy of fun or happiness, a grown-up plot designed to drown out joy and inspiration.

It's really not that at all. Discipline is also more than just hard work, but that's where the process starts. Ever since I can remember, I have been extremely organized and hardworking, whether I was helping my sisters clean the house, playing sports, doing well in school, modeling, or, even today, being a wife and working mother. Which is why I feel such a strong connection with this first lesson: *It all starts with discipline.* I believe that whatever success I've achieved in my life is the result of focus, hard work, dedication, being on time, doing what is necessary, what was asked of me, and always giving 100 percent to everything I did—and I still approach my life this way. In other words, discipline.

In our house, discipline mattered. With six children, all girls chattering away at the same time, it was a necessity. My mom, for one, was always running around, working as hard as she could to take care of all of us. Every morning at six a.m., she woke up and made us breakfast shakes using avocados or bananas or apples that she mixed with milk and a little bit of sugar, or sometimes she made us *torradas*, which are sandwiches with melted cheese inside. Afterward, she or my dad would drop us off at school, and my mom would go to work, coming back home at noontime so we could all eat lunch together. On weekends she got up even earlier to wash our clothes and to make and freeze meals for the week ahead.

With eight people sharing three bedrooms and two bathrooms,

The day Pati and I were born, July 20, 1980. My sisters and my maternal grandmother came to meet us.

We always took family photos in front of the Christmas tree in one corner of our house. *Top, left to right:* Raque and my twin sister, Pati. *Bottom, left to right:* my grandfather on my dad's side, Walter; Gabi; Fofa; me with my mouth open; and my paternal grandmother, Lucilla holding baby Fafi.

my sisters and I understood early on that we were expected to help out. Each of us was given a cleaning assignment before we were allowed to go outside and play. When Raque or Fofa rang the bell, it was off to our stations. I was usually in charge of cleaning the bathroom and often I spent a long time scrubbing between the tiles with a toothbrush until you could have eaten a meal off the floor. To be comfortable I've always needed my living spaces to be clean and organized. If my surroundings are messy, I can't even think properly. My sisters and I also each served as the unofficial "mom" for the sister just below us in age. At age eight, I remember changing my sister Fafi's diapers, and then helping my older sisters fry up empanadas in the kitchen that we'd helped our mom make from scratch—dough folded and sealed over fillings like chicken, beef, or cheese and spinach.

Good girl, my parents used to tell us whenever my sisters and I did something well. When we were polite. When we did what we were asked. When we worked hard, got good grades, or played a good volleyball game. But even when things didn't go according to plan, my mom and dad always made us feel we'd done the best we could if we applied ourselves and worked hard. *Good girl* was a big compliment. It always made me feel proud of the effort I'd put in.

Whether I was scrubbing bathroom tiles, studying hard to do well in school, or playing sports, I always brought an intense focus and motivation to everything I did. At age ten, when I started playing volleyball, I told myself that to get good at it, I needed to practice at least two hours a day. I decided I would train as hard as possible to make the team, and maybe the team one grade above mine. The way I approached schoolwork was no different. If I wasn't strong in a subject, I would stay up all night studying if necessary until I got an A. Discipline was never a faraway idea or something I'd grow into later in life. It was always a part of me—doing my best, making my parents proud, not letting anybody down. If I wanted to succeed at something, I wouldn't just envision what I wanted, or wait for it to show up, or expect someone to hand it to me. I knew I had to *do the work to make it happen*. Even if I was scared and it felt impossible. I always gave 100 percent of my effort because if I gave anything less than my best, I knew I'd get upset with myself. Yet underlying my sense of discipline was the strong feeling that whatever it was I set out to accomplish, I could do it if I worked hard enough. Even when I was afraid, I never felt defeated. I felt *challenged*.

As time went on, I became more disciplined, probably because I could see direct results. At age fourteen, when I left my hometown and family to move to São Paulo to pursue a career in modeling, I was determined. I told myself, *I'm not going to go back home empty-handed. I'm not going to disappoint my parents and my sisters. I'm going to work as hard as I can and do what I have to do, even if that means working all day and all night.* Without discipline, I might have taken the next bus home. The work could be intense, and I missed my family. Often I was lonely. But I stayed in São Paulo and kept at it.

My friend Maqui, me, my friend Karina, and my sister Pati in our *paquitas* outfits just before our performance at Horizontina's music festival, 1992.

One opportunity appeared, followed by another, and then another. I kept pushing myself.

By 1999, after I signed a contract with Victoria's Secret, I was working 350 days a year. During a typical season, just one day included modeling in up to six shows, followed by the fittings for the next day's shows. Hair and makeup could start at six a.m. and the fittings at times lasted until dawn. It didn't matter if I got to bed at two a.m. the night before—I needed to do fittings. *I showed up every morning on time.* It really wasn't a very glamorous scene. Only rarely did anyone offer me a glass of water, and some people felt free to be

Inside a little boat going to shoot the commercial in the middle of the icebergs in Iceland, 1998. It was freezing!

critical to my face. In my teens and twenties, I remember meeting one beautiful model after another—there were so many. I could barely believe it when, somehow, I was the one who ended up getting hired for many of the jobs. Why? I have to believe that discipline played a big role. I worked very hard, but I also tried to be fun to be around. All jobs are collaborations, and modeling is no different. I was never late—not once. I was 100 percent committed. One time on a job in Iceland, I was told to stand on a floating fake iceberg in the middle of a glacier, wearing only a string dress. I was freezing, and afraid I might slip and fall into the frigid water, and yet I just smiled, doing my best not to show how panicked I felt. I told myself that it didn't matter if I was shivering or if my lips were turning blue. I was going to do the job well.

I truly was just happy to be there! I felt so appreciative for every opportunity I was given. Why wouldn't anyone doing what I was doing feel like the luckiest person alive, even when pressed up against a glacier? Plus, I do believe that one reason I became good at modeling is that I wasn't naturally photogenic. There are lots of models who look fantastic on film. But I felt I wouldn't look good just standing in front of the camera. I had to become animated, more like an actress or a dancer, in order to create a special moment. It was important for me to do my job well, but also to never let modeling define who I was. I actually never *became* a model; I *did* modeling. Typically I'd work all day, and then go home to cuddle with my dog, Vida, and read. I wasn't interested in parties, glamour, fancy clothes, or late nights. I was happiest going home and starting a new book.

These days, when I can, I still do modeling jobs. I love to work. I love being creative, and my work offers me so many opportunities to learn. I love learning, and taking advantage of new experiences is part of my nature. But it hasn't always been easy, and it certainly wasn't a straight shot. Today I take *nothing* for granted—I never have. I plan to keep working hard and continue to give everything I do 100 percent. It's the only way I know how to be.

I believe if you want to succeed, there are four fundamental steps—or at least this has been true for me. Clarity comes first.

Everything in life starts with a dream. But first the dream needs to be clearly defined and, more important, you need to understand why you want it. At fourteen, and at twenty, and at twenty-seven, I never said to myself, "My goal is to be a great model." Rather, my emphasis was *to be the best at what I do, which means giving my best.* Honestly, I could have been in any number of professions! Still, whatever I ended up doing, I knew I would have to be the best at it. Not the best compared with others, but the best version of *myself.*

In my experience, clearly defining what you want gives you direction and the inner fire that can motivate you. Maybe you're a B student who wants to get As. Or maybe you want to be good at sports. A terrific wife and mother. Successful at your job. A great human being. Maybe you want to work out regularly or meditate every day. Then be very clear with yourself up front. How will reaching your goals serve a larger purpose? *Why* does it matter to you? What are you willing to do to come closer to achieving your goals? What do you need to get there?

It's also important to set reasonable expectations. I know from personal experience the danger of setting the bar too high and, if you do, how easy it is when you come up short to start criticizing yourself or feeling like a failure, when the truth is that you weren't being realistic.

Once you're clear about what you want to achieve, next is *focus*— taking the many small actions to propel yourself forward. This is where the hard-work part comes in. What will it take for you to reach that goal? Do you need to change your daily routine or eliminate certain behaviors, or even some people, from your life? If you're a B student who wants to get all As, it might mean that you start getting up an hour earlier to study, or ask for extra help from your teacher, or form a study group. You might also look for a mentor or role model who can show you the way.

The third step is *dedication*. This means staying on track over the long haul, and giving yourself credit for what you've done well, but also concentrating on those areas where you need improvement. *How* are you practicing? How are you measuring your own progress? Are you focusing on what you already do well, or are you also stretching yourself by targeting the things you may be less good at, and then trying some problem-solving? In my experience, hard work and dedication aren't the same thing. Dedication includes a commitment to a specific goal or ideal. A lot of people work incredibly hard, but some don't stick with the steps needed to achieve what it is they really want. You may set a number of goals for yourself, but without dedication they won't become realized. Who has a better chance of becoming a successful musician: the pianist who practices an hour a day or the one who practices four hours a day? Dedication means putting in the *time towards* what you want, and love, the areas where you want to achieve excellence. Dedication says, *I'm going to keep on going, no matter what.* Without dedication, you're less likely to see the benefits of all your hard work. If focus means saying yes to hard work,

I was in São Paulo in 1996, walking to Blockbuster Video in the rain, when I heard mewing. I brought the little cat home, hid him, and named him Fominha—Portuguese for "the one that eats everything"—since whatever I gave him he would devour in two seconds. When I learned I couldn't bring him to the United States, where I was moving a few months later, I made sure he found a good home.

dedication means saying no to distraction—to the activities and even the people pulling you in different directions or pushing you to give up. Be honest with yourself: What do you accomplish in a day? Is your time consumed by answering texts and emails? Are you making progress or just getting caught up? I kept putting one foot in front of the next, even when I was teased by my schoolmates, or felt homesick at age fourteen, or was rejected. I moved forward, one casting after another. Of course there were times when I missed my parents and my sisters terribly, but even though those moments were painful and distracting, they were only temporary visitors. They came and they went. At the same time, I wanted—I needed—to show myself that I could do what I set out to accomplish.

The fourth step, *humility*, is especially important to me. If you're clear, focused, and dedicated, and you end up succeeding at what you set out to do, you might believe you deserve special treatment. Well, you don't! Most people don't have an easy road to the top of any profession. We all face challenges along the way that force us to grow and learn. I know I am no exception. When any level of success is reached, that's the time to reflect on all your challenges. Yes, you may be unusual. Your skills and talents may make you stand out. You may work, as I do, in a public profession. Good for you! But, to my mind, the moment you start thinking you're better than anyone else, your achievements don't matter very much. You fall to the bottom rung of the ladder. But if you have humility, you achieve something more important than worldly success: you become a lifelong learner. Humility allows you to grow from your mistakes, to know that everyone and every experience can teach you *something*. In my experience, it opens the doors to a bigger, more meaningful life.

At the end of the day, how different are we from one another?

We're all students in the "School of Life" on this earth. Our campus is a tiny blue dot floating in space. And who are we, really, in the face of all this immensity?

In 2015, I took a step back from modeling, but that doesn't mean I stopped working. Today, in fact, I work almost as much as I always have, minus a lot of the traveling. The same discipline that has served me my whole life I now apply to being the best wife and mother I can be. My relationship to discipline has helped me create a daily routine, and yet I am constantly adapting it to fit the ever-changing details of my life.

Structure always helps me stay on track, especially now that I have small children. There are so many interruptions and unexpected events that would throw me if I *didn't* have a basic structure. I recognize that I'm lucky, because I have a support staff and most people don't have the day-to-day help that I get, but I still have a long list of details and activities that can't be delegated and demand my full attention.

After my second child was born, I realized I needed to craft a completely different kind of daily routine. My goal was to create time for every person and activity that was important to me. There are only twenty-four hours in a day. So I asked myself: *What should a schedule look like that would allow enough time for me, my husband, my children, and the many projects I wanted to do in the world?*

In order to supply the love and attention I need to give my children, my husband, my sisters, my friends, and even my dogs, I need to focus on my needs first. As a wife and a mom, I am the person in our house who sets the emotional tone of our family. If I'm not feeling good, or if I'm stressed out, or feeling unhappy, my whole family will be affected.

I wake up every morning anywhere between five a.m. and six a.m. to the "ocean" sound on my phone, which sits on my bedside table in Airplane Mode. It's a soothing way to begin my day. The sound of the water and the breaking waves fills me with a deep sense of peace. Also, I don't leap out of bed unless the kids wake me up before the water sounds begin. Instead I like to relax into the process of waking up, as if I'm tiptoeing into warm water. I stretch a little; take a few long, deep breaths, followed by a few minutes of appreciation for my life, my husband, my children, and my cozy bed. Tom gets up early, too, especially during football season, when most mornings he's already left the house for the stadium by six a.m.

The first thing I do in the morning is fetch a bottle of coconut oil from the bathroom, so I can do oil pulling. It's the ancient Ayurvedic technique of swishing oil in your mouth to clean out all the guck and to detoxify teeth and gums. It's supposed to be good for your overall gut health, too. I put one teaspoon of oil in my mouth and swish it around for ten or fifteen minutes. You can use many different kinds of oil—sesame, olive, sunflower—but I use organic coconut oil because I like the flavor. I continue oil pulling as I'm getting dressed, and I'm still swishing as I head downstairs to let the dogs out; then I spit.

After letting the dogs back in, I meditate. I light a candle, get into lotus position, and close my eyes. It doesn't really matter if you cross your legs. What matters is sitting tall with your spine straight so energy can flow. Before having children, I would go on retreats where I would sit in silence for a weekend or longer. Now, as I mentioned, because of my busy life I meditate every morning usually for just five minutes. This practice helps to support my inner balance for the rest of the day.

I've been meditating since 2003, so I can quickly get to a deep state of awareness. Sometimes I meditate to figure out the answer to a question. Or because I'm confused about an experience and need insight. For example, if I have an emotional knot in my stomach, or a cloudy mind that won't go away, meditation will help me understand why, and also what I need to do to find relief. Other times my goal is just to find peace or inner calm. Sometimes I switch things up. When Tom is home during the off-season, now and again I meditate in my own bed in the morning and, then again, before a business meeting, as it helps my mind to be clear and focused. If Tom and I are on vacation and the kids are with their babysitter, I'll meditate longer. Creating the space and time for meditation has provided me answers. Some people might see meditation as a waste of time. I see it as an exercise in focus and clarity. As a result, I am actually saving time. Today I do my best to bring the positive energy I feel during my meditation practice into my everyday life, to be present and aware of each

Benny, meditating with me during a full moon in Costa Rica, 2014.

moment and passing thought. This can happen while I'm working out, taking a walk, or eating a meal. Some days are better than others, but the idea is to keep on practicing, knowing that it will get easier.

My preference is to do my workout soon after waking up, since my day gets busier as it goes. If I'm working out at home, I put on my Bluetooth earphones and go on the elliptical while listening to a book on tape, or sometimes I'll listen to the audio of a YouTube video on a subject that fascinates me—say, a series about ancient Egypt or Greece. If I've dropped the kids off at school—Benny is now eight and Vivi is five—sometimes I'll drive to the TB12 Sports Therapy Center in Foxboro, about half an hour south of our home in Boston, so I can do rehab for my shoulders and knee. I have dislocated my shoulders a number of times, and last year I tore my ACL while skiing.

As with every aspect in life, my morning routine doesn't always go as planned. Some days I'm completely exhausted. I don't *want* to get up early to meditate and work out because I got to bed too late or because one of my kids had a nightmare or a fever and slept beside me all night. Sometimes Tom won't get home from away games until one a.m. and an hour later the kids pile onto our bed. Tom's games can be emotionally draining. I'm sitting in the stands watching three-hundred-pound guys crash into the man I love, and it's not a movie; it's the reality of my husband's life. That's why I must stay flexible and some mornings I tell myself, *Okay, you're not going to meditate first thing. You can meditate after lunch.* Meditation is a tool. It's there to support me in being my best, not to trap me or punish me, and on some mornings, sleeping an extra half hour is the best thing I can do for myself. On other days when Benny and Vivi are up very early, I just take a few minutes with them to gaze outside at the sun rising up over the hills. We all love sun gazing.

After meditating and working out, I drink a glass of lukewarm water, about eight ounces, with half a slice of lemon squeezed into it. It helps flush out the digestive system. As I sip my lemon water, I'm busy making my children's breakfasts and school lunches. I believe strongly in the old saying "Let food be thy medicine," and I take nutrition seriously. For lunch I'll pack Benny and Vivi hummus or lentil soup or leftover rice and beans. I'll add diced cucumber, avocado, or chickpeas to the rice to liven it up. Or some days I'll make burritos, Benny's favorite, with a few sprinkles of cheese on top. Then I fill up the kids' water bottles, along with a few drops of my husband's electrolytes. I always try to create as little trash or waste as possible, especially in the form of plastic bottles and bags. My goal is to live as lightly as possible, and I never throw anything away as long as it can have another use. I will compost it, reuse it, or recycle it.

Breakfast is often hectic, with kids chattering, dogs roaming, and a tight schedule. I often make Benny and Vivi gluten-free toast with almond butter and honey, or eggs with sliced avocado, or a bowl of cut-up apples and berries with coconut yogurt. Before breakfast, Benny and Vivi do their chores. Benny feeds the dogs (I'm the one who puts the food in the bowls, otherwise Benny would feel sorry for them and give them too much), and then he and Vivi set the table. After breakfast, the kids put their dishes in the sink. If there's time, Benny goes off and plays with his LEGOs and Vivi plays with her toy ponies or sometimes they like playing chase around the house, especially when their brother, Jack, is with them. I finish cleaning up the kitchen counter, since I like leaving rooms as tidy as I found them, plus, as I said before, I can't think straight if I'm in a messy environment. Then I eat my own breakfast. Often I finish off my kids' leftovers, or drink a glass of green juice with celery, cucumbers, half a

Benny and Vivi on their first day back to school after the Christmas break, 2016. Look at those cute faces!

red or green apple, turmeric, ginger, lemon juice, and sometimes kale or beets, or I have avocado toast. Benny and Vivi pick up their backpacks, zip their jackets, and put on their shoes. Then we're off.

The car ride to school is one of my favorite times of the day. It's just the three of us, Benny and Vivi in the backseat and me behind the wheel. We love singing in the car, though Benny takes his singing very seriously and doesn't like it when Vivi sings at the same time, so if he's singing, she plays the part of deejay. On the drive back, I listen to a podcast or an audiotape or sometimes an astrology report.

If I wasn't able to do my workout earlier, I do it when I get back from taking the kids to school. Afterward, I take a quick shower, and now I'm truly ready to start my day.

I usually don't wear makeup if I am working from home, but if I go out I like to wear at least some lip balm, a light mascara, and a little bit of concealer, and in my bag you will always find concealer and tinted lip balm. Do I sometimes enjoy wearing makeup? Absolutely. It's a fantastic tool. If I look half-asleep, or I have circles under my eyes or a pimple on my face, or I want to make my eyes pop, concealer and mascara are best friends. Makeup is fun. It's the only way my eyes will ever look large, or at least not small. Which is why if I'm going to a public event, I always wear makeup.

But I don't think about wearing makeup as an *obligation*. The truth is, I think looking good and having good skin has more to do with what you eat, how you live, and how you feel. (Having a good dermatologist can also help.) I do think that I look my best when I eat healthy, exercise every day, drink plenty of fluids, and get the rest that my brain and body need. Our insides reflect our outsides, and vice versa. If we maintain a healthy inner environment, it will show up in our complexions—and to me, nothing could be more naturally beautiful.

But back to my day. After my early-morning routine, I feel energized, my mind is clear, and I'm ready to sit at my laptop and focus 100 percent on being productive. I keep a separate space a short distance across the lawn from our house. I call it the Sanctuary. I love it. It's clean and quiet and sparsely decorated, with plants, crystals, high ceilings, and lots of light. I spend most of the day there answering emails and phone calls and having meetings. Often in the mornings I am in close contact with my twin sister, Pati, and Fafi, discussing business, evaluating new opportunities, approving material for clients, answering interview questions, or working on environmental projects. Today, most of the companies I work with are in Brazil, and I consistently express my concerns about our environment, and the need to create products and practices that are sustainable for the earth. Some companies are definitely more conscious of sustainability than others and are making changes to clean up their supply chains. I hope in the future that caring for our environment will become a priority for companies across all industries. Although I've been working in my industry for a long time, it wasn't until recently that I learned that the fashion industry, especially fast fashion, is one of the biggest polluters on the earth, and that most clothes end up in landfills. I am now using my voice and contacts to bring attention to this problem, and to develop solutions to make the business of fashion more sustainable. For almost ten years, I've also been working as a Goodwill Ambassador for the United Nations Environmental Programme, in order to help draw attention to environmental issues. This opportunity has been a tremendous learning experience. I've traveled abroad and met so many inspiring people from different parts of the world who are developing innovative solutions to the problems in their communities. I love learning and sharing experiences and knowledge with the wide variety of people I meet. I connect with experts and like-minded people who have the same desire to do their part to make the world a better place, like my friends and colleagues at Believe Earth, the project that some friends in Brazil and I started to bring more awareness to the preservation of our planet. Part of our mission is to share inspiring stories of ordinary people who are making a difference in the lives of their communities as a way to inspire more people to work for the greater good. My days are extremely full—and never quite long enough. I really wish each day could be forty-eight hours long!

I often have a number of different projects going at once. During the day I keep the ringer of my cell phone turned off. Of course I check it regularly to see if Tom or someone from my kids' school has called, but in general anyone who knows me knows I dislike talking on the phone. I prefer seeing people up close, face-to-face. When I'm traveling, I FaceTime Tom and the kids every day, but when I'm at home, I refuse to be a slave to my phone. During meals, a big rule in our family is no gadgets at the table!

I leave the Sanctuary and head back to the house in the middle of the day for lunch—usually a fresh salad or a big bowl of soup. Lunch is also when I get a handle on whatever issues may have come up that morning with the children, babysitters, house stuff, and so forth. An hour later I'm back in the Sanctuary, where I work until late afternoon. I drink water all day long, as well as lots of tea. My favorites are lemongrass, chamomile, and mint, ideally made with fresh chamomile and mint leaves from my own little garden. But it all depends on how I'm feeling. If I'm getting sick, for example, I'll drink fennel tea, or prepare a honey-lemon-ginger concoction on the stove. Otherwise I always drink my tea straight, without honey or sugar.

By the late afternoon, Renata, our babysitter, has picked up Benny and Vivi from school, and from now on it's all about my family. I make it a point to talk to Renata in front of Benny and Vivi so that they know we talk about them—and to teach them not to treat me one way and her another. Sometimes I run a bath for the kids, or else they take a shower, and then it's time for dinner, with Benny and Vivi usually helping set the table. During the football season, Tom is home by six p.m. unless he's playing an away game, and our dinners usually last about an hour. I always ask Tom about his day, but usually the conversation revolves around the kids. After dinner we usually FaceTime Jack, Tom's son from a previous relationship who I call my bonus child, to check how he's doing and say good night. If Jack is visiting, he takes his older-brother status seriously. Benny always wants to make everyone laugh. Vivi is the one who laughs the hardest, and who clearly loves her two brothers. She is their greatest cheerleader, and wants to feel she's part of the gang.

After dinner the kids vanish to watch Portuguese cartoons on TV, which gives Tom and me some alone time to talk about our day, sometimes over another cup of chamomile tea. Both Benny and Vivi speak fluent Portuguese, Benny with a slight accent and Vivi as if she were born in Brazil. Jack is understanding Portuguese more and more, and I love it when he tries to speak, because his accent is so

The kids watching Daddy play, Foxborough, 2017.

cute. When I was growing up, my parents spoke German exclusively to each other, though never to us, as they wanted to keep whatever they said between them. Today, after years of traveling, I've become fairly fluent in four languages. Benny and Vivi may be American and born in Boston, but they're Brazilian, too. Neither of my parents speaks English all that well, and my nieces and one of my sisters don't speak English at all, and it's important to me that my children are able to communicate with my family. So every summer I take Benny and Vivi on a two-week holiday with my entire family where we speak only Portuguese. I like to think I'm raising my children to be citizens of the world. I also believe that the more we can talk to people in their own language, the more we will understand one another.

When I think about my daily schedule, I realize that almost every moment of the day feels like a ritual and I really want to create a series of special small moments. It's up to all of us to capture time, to give it meaning, and to be present and appreciative for every moment we're alive. This is why making a big deal out of little moments matters a lot to me. Stretching my body the moment I wake up. Being conscious of my breath. Lighting a candle. Meditating. Singing with my kids on our way to school. More than anything, these moments are about appreciation. My goal is to *be present.* To feel and experience my life deeply, even if what I'm feeling overwhelms me or sometimes makes me burst into tears (which I do now and then). To live a full and meaningful life with the awareness of what's happening around me—and to inspire my children to live that way, too.

Bedtime is another ritual. When Tom is home, he kisses the kids good night and sometimes he tells them a story. At bedtime, I love reading out loud to each child. Then I do something I've done since Benny and Vivi were infants: I give them each a quick foot massage using aromatherapy oils, of which I have an entire pharmacy. Five minutes of foot rubbing really calms them down, and makes us feel close.

The last thing I do before saying good night is to remind them to pray to their guardian angel. I often wait outside their rooms, listening to them saying their prayers, and it melts my heart every time.

I generally fall asleep later than Tom. During football season, Tom likes to be in bed by nine p.m. After brushing my teeth and reading a few pages of a book, I check my phone to see if there's anything urgent, slip it into Airplane Mode, and reset my wake-up alarm.

That's my day. It varies if I'm traveling in Brazil or New York or on the West Coast, or sometimes even when I'm in Boston. If I'm in another city for a photo shoot, I carry out some variation of the same routine. I get up at six a.m., meditate, and work out, even if it's for only twenty minutes, because I know that as the day goes on, the less motivated I'll be to exercise; and after a long day of work at the studio, I know it won't happen. If I'm doing TV commercial work, the day can go as long as twelve hours. If I'm doing magazine work, it lasts anywhere from eight to ten hours. As I said, I check my phone rarely when I'm working, though as soon as I'm done, I always FaceTime Tom and the kids. Before going to bed I like to take a shower, especially if they used lots of product and my hair looks crazy. I am usually under the covers no later than ten p.m. I need at least seven hours of sleep, eight if I can get it. Thankfully I've never had any trouble falling asleep. I'm usually exhausted at night, and as soon as I put my head on the pillow, I am gone.

People often tell themselves stories to explain who they are and how they got that way. One of my stories is that I developed my work ethic from sharing a small house with five sisters and from watching my parents work as hard as they did. Another one I tell comes from being a middle child (and a twin on top of that), who never felt all that special and who never wanted to disappoint her parents, which turned into a desire to not disappoint *herself*.

There's truth to both of those stories, but I also know that being disciplined, and being *intense* about that discipline, is just who I am. I think I was born that way. Even if I did grow up as one of six sisters, to parents who worked very hard, and even if I pushed myself to do well in school and in sports, those things were just arenas where I could test and play out a trait already inside me. Joseph Campbell once wrote, "You become mature when you become the authority of your own life." In my case, for whatever reasons I took on that authority starting when I was young. When I tell people I never wanted to let my parents down, that was true—it still is—but what I'm really saying is that I never wanted to fall short of my *own* expectations.

If discipline doesn't come easily, what's the best way to create it? It begins with self-awareness, and self-awareness is a process. It's not something we're born with. It's something we develop over time. I know this much: the better you know yourself, and what you're good at, and what brings you joy, the easier it is to focus on what you want to manifest—which in turn makes it easier for you to manifest what you want. What *do* you want? What works best for *you*? Are you at your best at a certain hour, on a certain kind of day, in a certain environment? Do you make it a point to expose yourself to positive words, positive images, inspiring people, inspiring ideas? If you spend all day on your phone, for example, reading the news, and making yourself anxious or scared, or if you set unfair goals for yourself, I believe you're setting yourself up for failure and unhappiness. As I said, if I tell myself I'm going to meditate in the morning for thirty minutes but every day I get interrupted, the problem isn't my children wanting their breakfast, or the dogs wanting to go outside; it's *me* being unrealistic about what's going on around me!

I think of discipline as the voice of a parent or an authority figure inside us. It keeps us answerable for our actions. But if that voice isn't strong enough inside you, consider creating a parent on the *out-side*. Find another way to track your progress, to keep yourself accountable. This is something I've done with my own children. Vivi and Benny are very young and still have a lot to learn. (Who doesn't? I know I do.) To help them organize their routine, and to give them tasks and responsibilities, the solution we came up with was a whiteboard.

The board hangs in our kitchen. It replaced one that had actual magnetic stars on it, but when Vivi began gaming the system and covering her side of the board with as many stars as could fit, we found one with a black pen and an eraser. The board first appeared during a short-lived stage when Benny started talking back to me. Whenever I'd ask him to do anything, his attitude was that I knew nothing, and even if I did, I was wrong. So Tom and I decided to address the situation head-on. I told Benny it was okay if he got angry or frustrated about the rules we set, but he couldn't treat me disrespectfully. If he was mad at me, he had to tell me. Benny admitted that he wasn't always nice to me, and he said that he was sorry. Then he came up with the idea of the whiteboard.

Here's how it works. When we notice that the kids need more structure, we ask them questions at dinner. How were their manners? Did they say "please" and "thank you"? Did they look their friends and teachers in the eye when talking to them? Were they kind to their friends and to each other? If they had a friend over that day, did they tidy up their bedrooms and put away their toys afterward? After meals, did they bring their dishes over to the sink? When I asked them to do something, did they do it? If the answer to the question is *yes*, the child who answered it gets a star.

Stars can be given, but they can also be withheld. If Benny, say, pinched his sister, or if Vivi forgot to be a good hostess during her playdate, they don't get a star. Instead we talk about the things they can keep working at, whether it's being a better listener or working on their patience. We keep a list of expectations on the board so they understand that everything is a work in progress. The star system has really helped. Even better, the kids are becoming much more at ease with their emotions and with who they are as people. Benny will tell us that he ate a cookie before dinner, for example, and also that he's afraid I will get angry. Yes, he'll lose a star, but rather than getting mad, I thank him for being truthful, which encourages him to be honest. What matters most to me is that we've helped create an environment where our kids feel safe to express their feelings and to have real conversations, and that they know that their dad and I are walking with them, side by side, but not carrying them. I remind my kids that we are all learning together. I'm thirty-eight years old! I've never been a parent before! As much as it's my job to teach them, they're also teaching *me*. So what are some of the things *I* could be doing better?

We try to give our children what we got from our own parents growing up. If we're lucky, we get to fill in parts that, for whatever reason, were left blank for us. When I was growing up in Horizontina, there were six of us girls at the dinner table, six voices rising up to talk or laugh or disagree at once. One day my dad made a rule: if one of us had something to say, we needed to raise our hand. With all those children, my mom also didn't have time to read us books before bed. She hardly had a second to herself. Sometimes I would get up in the middle of the night and see her at the kitchen table, still working, a calculator with rolls of paper billowing out of it in front of her, trying to make the figures add up. Raque, Fofa, Pati, Gabi, Fafi, and

I had to figure out a lot of things by ourselves. In some ways, we were children raising children. We had to learn how to negotiate. How to agree. How to fight fairly. But never once during my childhood did I ever feel that I was missing out, or that I lacked anything at all. How could I lack or miss out on something I never knew existed? I felt, and still do, that I had the best childhood in the world!

I'm aware that my circumstances today are different from the ones faced by my parents. The job I began working at when I was fourteen, and over the next twenty-three years, allows me more time for my children. I can read to them, massage their feet, teach them how to breathe and how to express their feelings. I can capture as many fast-moving moments as I can while there's still time and experience them *as* they happen.

In 2017, I was asked to give the opening speech at Rock in Rio in front of an audience of around 100,000 people. For people who don't know it, Rock in Rio is one of the biggest music festivals in the world. Over the years it has featured acts like Beyoncé, Prince, Rihanna, George Michael, REM, the Red Hot Chili Peppers, Dave Matthews Band, Coldplay, and U2. The call came right around the same time that the president of Brazil, Michel Temer, announced that the government had abolished an enormous national reserve in the Amazon (RENCA) in order to open up the region for mining. As many as nine natural environmental and indigenous reserves would be negatively affected. I've been working on the protection of the environment since 2004, when I visited the Amazon and saw up close how the indigenous Indian tribes, especially young children and elderly people, were getting poisoned and even dying because of the pesticides and the mercury in the river where they bathed and fished. My heart was heavy when I saw this reality. I saw firsthand how environmental toxins were directly affecting their lives, but the truth of the matter is that contaminated water and soil affect all of us. As far as I'm concerned, any attack on nature is an attack on all of life. As a mother and a nurturer, my natural instinct is to protect. My reaction to the Brazilian president's new law was outrage, followed closely by, *I have to do something. We can't let this happen.* A group of us put up such a protest on social media that the Brazilian government said it was going to postpone the discussion to another time, subject to an extended debate.

When Marcos, a friend of mine and one of the co-creators of Believe Earth, who knew Roberto Medina, the creator of Rock in Rio, asked me to open the concert, I said yes. But I hung up the phone feeling terrified. I'd never given a speech in front of 100,000 people. I'd never even *written* a speech as important as this one. A few minutes later I became aware of something inside me. Determination. *Discipline.* If something was scaring me, I knew it was up to me, only me, to work through my fear. If I wanted to succeed, I had to do the work. A big part of me wanted nothing more than to stay home and be safe. I also worried that since the audience was coming to Rock in Rio to hear music—Ivete Sangalo, Maroon 5, The Who, and Guns N' Roses were all performing that year—they'd get angry when I came out to give a speech. *What if they don't listen to me?* I thought. *Or boo me, or yell at me, or throw things at me? It doesn't matter,* was my next thought. *Get out of your own head. Just do it. If you don't stand up for what you care about, then you're complicit.*

It didn't matter that I'd never written a speech in my life. It didn't matter how long I had to sit there in front of my laptop before the words came out. It didn't matter how frightened I was, or how stupid I might look, or the hundred other reasons why it was a bad idea to put myself in this situation. I became aware that for now and forever, my bigger purpose was *love*. It wasn't about me. I was speaking in service to a cause more important than myself. I was being tested, and one of the tests involved courage. It wasn't the first time I'd appeared in public before an audience that size. I'd walked the longest runway of my life (more than four hundred feet) at the opening ceremony of the 2016 Rio Olympics before hundreds of millions of people watching on television, an experience that also terrified me—before I did it. That night I remember feeling like a speck of light being carried by the energy of the crowd. But Rock in Rio would be different. At the Olympics I could sense the audience, but the stadium was so dark I wouldn't be able to see anyone. Plus, this time, instead of walking, I had to talk. I knew Rock in Rio wouldn't be easy for me, even if I'd appeared in front of a big audience before. Because let's face it, talking is a much bigger responsibility than walking!

But, if I hadn't done the walk, I couldn't have done the talk. Remembering that helped steady my confidence. I believe that when you face a challenge, you have to rise up to meet it. Then the next challenge that appears is a little harder, but then you rise up to meet *that* one. Isn't that how we grow? When I got to the end of my speech, I wrote: *When we can dream, when we're able to imagine . . . we can create a better world.* I wanted to end with a song, since I was at a rock festival after all, but what song? My sister Fafi, who was sitting next to me, said, "What about 'Imagine' by John Lennon? Doesn't that sound like the message you've been writing about and want to communicate?" Right then I knew that "Imagine" would be the perfect song to conclude my speech. Also, how incredible would it be if Ivete Sangalo, one of the most popular singers in Brazil, who is not only an amazing musician but also a dear friend, a wonderful woman, and a beautiful human being, could begin singing the song when I was done speaking? When I found out that Ivete would be coming on-stage right after me as one of the concert's headliners, I called her and told her I needed her help. "I'm with you!" Ivete said. I was so excited! Everything was coming together.

The night of the festival, my emotions were all over the place. Before I went onstage, the woman in charge of the event tried to be helpful. She told me, "Don't worry, even Bono and Coldplay get nervous when they play here." Funny, but hearing that only made me *more* nervous. So I took a moment for myself. I closed my eyes. I took the time to create an intention. I asked God, *Please allow the audience to feel what I'm feeling. Let them feel my heart.* I wanted to connect with them. I wanted them to feel that we are all connected, all one. It gave me a rush, a strength, and the confidence I needed to go on. Then I went out on the big stage.

I talked for several minutes. I didn't talk about the Amazon, or about mining, or about any other problems facing the country. Not directly, that is. Instead I talked about the power of the collective, and about hope, and about all of us standing together. At one point my emotions overtook me, and I started crying. Then Ivete appeared. She gave me a big hug and started singing. She'd asked me to sing with her, and though I hadn't planned on it—I'd felt too shy—when the moment came, I couldn't help it. It was more karaoke-style singing on my part than anything else, especially when you find yourself duetting with a singer like Ivete. And "Imagine" did the rest of the talking.

What can ever prepare you for something like that? There's no manual. There's no rulebook. You just do it. You put aside your fears. You tell yourself nothing is going to stop you. A night like that is no different from any mountain you know you have to climb, so you lace up your boots and you climb the mountain. You learn from the experience of doing it. When the next mountain appears, you're a little better, a little sharper, a little more practiced at making your way to the top.

That's how discipline has served me my whole life. It hasn't just helped me accomplish what I set out to do. It's helped me see how I can do *more*. I just have to trust myself and go for it.

If anything, I remind myself sometimes that I need to relax my own sense of discipline and to be gentler and more compassionate with myself. To some people, I probably might come off as a little obsessive or overly driven. I'm working on it—and becoming a parent has made me much more forgiving with myself. Once I was someone for whom nothing was good enough. *I* wasn't good enough. In 2015, when Taschen published a book to celebrate my twenty-three years in fashion, I remember Giovanni Bianco, the book's art director, asking me, "Gisele, when did you have time to go to the bathroom? It's so obvious that for years you didn't have a life!"

He was right. Back then I *didn't* have much of a life. It was only when I started going through the thousands of photos to select the three hundred or so that appeared in the book that I finally got a sense of just how hard I'd worked. I feel appreciation many times a day, but those photos jogged my memory in other ways. For the first time I could see just how far a middle twin from a small village in southern Brazil had come. I remembered all the people I met, all the conversations I had, all the feelings I felt, all the countries I visited. For the first time ever I gave myself a pat on the back. *You did okay,* I thought. *You did it. You made it to the other side. And today, you're not only sane, you're stronger, wiser, and more confident.*

Good girl.

2

Challenges Are
Opportunities in Disguise

I've always been an intuitive person. When I left home, I usually had a pretty good sense of how to stay safe and make wise choices. Yet like everyone, I've had circumstances in my life that weren't going well. Sometimes an event or a situation occurred that simply was unacceptable—a conflict or a confrontation—and then I had no choice but to change. Our relationships help us grow because they mirror the best and worst of ourselves. When I reflect on my life, I can clearly see that the times that I've learned the most and made the most positive changes have also been the most difficult times. These were situations when I made poor choices—but I question whether they really were "mistakes" or rather, just experiences and opportunities to learn. Today I'm convinced that every challenge I've ever faced turned out in the end to be an opportunity in disguise, one that in time lifted me to a better place, making me more aware, and also stronger.

A typical day for me in New York City in 1997—on my flip phone, about to board the subway to a day of castings.

Inevitably when I think back to a time in my early twenties, I remember that I felt so helpless that I questioned whether I wanted to live.

I was on a hamster wheel, and yet I didn't even know it. I was twenty-three years old, successful at what I did, and working 350 days a year. My life consisted of getting aboard airplanes and flying to different locations and studios all over the world. I rarely unpacked my suitcases—I just swapped my dirty clothes for clean ones, got back on the next plane, then turned around and did the same thing again two days later, and again three days after that. I began my mornings with a mocha Frappuccino with whipped cream, along with the first of that day's pack of cigarettes. As for food, at that time I never gave any thought to what I put inside my body. Working in Japan when I was in my teens had introduced me to eating quickly and on the run. At night when I came home to my New York apartment, I hung up my coat, and poured myself a glass of wine. Afterwards I still felt too wired from all the coffee and nicotine I'd had that day and I needed something more to help me relax. What could be more natural than to polish off the rest of the wine bottle as I read a book or caught up on phone calls? I was a workaholic. In those days I was living the opposite of a healthy lifestyle.

I was living 100 miles per hour, smoking, drinking, eating badly, not sleeping much, and living pretty much out of a suitcase. It was

With my sister Gabi in Paris in my hotel room, having room service at the end of a busy show season, October 1999.

intense! I was in transit all the time, either heading off or coming back from somewhere, which meant I never felt grounded or settled—or took the time to think about my life. It was just my life. And like a lot of people in their early twenties, I felt indestructible.

Along with not knowing I was on a hamster wheel, I didn't understand that I was also basically relying on stimulants and depressants to get me through the day. Coffee to get me going in the morning. Cigarettes to punctuate the long hours and create a space for me at work without anyone—stylists, hair people, makeup people—touching me. Steak, burgers, french fries, pasta, pizza, candy, and whatever else to keep up my energy. Red wine to relax me and help me fall asleep.

I didn't have my first drink until I was nineteen, but champagne was always available before a show. Very few designers offered any food for the models, which is why anytime I spied food backstage, I filled my bag with it. After a while it became my signature "thing" to go around giving out whatever snacks I had—sandwiches, crackers, candy—to the other models, most of whom, like me, had spent all day galloping from show to show, forgetting to eat. As I said, my life back then was go, go, go all the time. During show season it was normal for me to wake up at five a.m. and not go to bed until one or two a.m., since after finishing work, as mentioned earlier, I still had to do fittings for the next day's shows and then the shows after that. If I did the whole circuit—in those days London, Milan, Paris, and New York—it was a marathon that would last a month. Invariably I got sick toward the end, but not wanting to disappoint anyone, I pushed through, to the point of once almost fainting in the middle of the runway, and another time, getting so sick I had to fly home for a few days before the season ended.

Looking back, I now see that I'd gone so numb I couldn't see what was happening. I was literally killing myself. I was poisoning my body from the moment I woke up in the morning to the moment I crashed at night. I was also creating a ripe environment for developing an anxiety problem. When you're nineteen years old, maybe you can get away with working 350 days a year, but by the time you're twenty-three and have been running on overdrive for years, well, your body, mind, and soul begin breaking down. I was trying my best to cope with the realities of my life.

What happened caught me by surprise, considering all the things I'd seen up to that point in my industry and all the traps I'd managed to avoid. When I left home at fourteen, obviously I was still very young, but for whatever reason I felt grown up and able to deal with adult challenges in my new adult world. Somehow I had always felt protected. I also knew that every decision I made affected me directly. I couldn't rely on my parents either. I was working all over the world, and my mom and dad were back home in Horizontina. Now as a mother to small children, I can only imagine the worry my parents must have gone through. I am not sure they would even have let me go if they knew how crazy the world outside our small town could be.

So many young female models seemed to be living in a hell that, as far as I could tell, they were unconsciously helping to create. Girls my own age, out of control at clubs, taking drugs, heading into dark places. I could have easily been one of them: another model taking the two-free-drink chits and the ecstasy tablet from the guy standing outside the nightclub. But that was never me. As I said, something or someone always protected me. It might have been the voice of my mom, who, before I left home, told me never, ever to accept anything, especially drinks, from strangers. In Tokyo, night after night I saw the same thing—teams of girls going out to clubs and getting wasted, and guys taking advantage of them. The whole time I felt like an observer, detached, as if I were looking at everything that was happening through a lens or a sheet of glass. Sometimes as I walked to the subway on my way to work in the early morning, past groups of little black birds nibbling the garbage on the sidewalks, I'd see girls coming back from the clubs, looking sick and disoriented. I didn't understand how they could function. If staying away from that scene made me an outsider, fine; it wasn't a path I wanted to go down. If my roommate and I *did* go to a club, I'd order a soda while she flirted with the bartender she had a crush on. Afterward I'd walk home and read a book. Clubbing, drinking, taking drugs, and staying out late never seemed to me like a very smart choice. I knew I would feel bad, people would take advantage of me, and I'd end up feeling broken. It wasn't for me. Also, my parents trusted me. They'd let me leave home

My twin sister, Pati, and I celebrating our twenty-first birthday with strawberry margaritas at a restaurant in New Paltz, New York, near my cabin in Woodstock.

so I could have a shot at this modeling thing, and I didn't want to do anything to disappoint them. I wanted them to be proud of me, and I also wanted to be a good example to my sisters.

I enjoyed modeling, too—all the opportunities I was given to see the world and meet different, fascinating people. I also loved being able to shape-shift. Fashion is so varied. It's changeable and playful. Fake lashes and push-up bras one day, latex clothes and wigs the next, a string bikini and a bayonet the day after. It was like doing experiments on my identity: *Who will I be today?* Fashion appealed to my sense of limitlessness. I've never liked anyone defining me or telling me I'm this or I'm that. *You're a model. Sit down. Don't say anything. Just be pretty.* To my mind I can be anything I *want* to be, and not one of those things involves being static or mute. The hard parts about modeling were the constant traveling, the promotional obligations including the launch parties, and the fact that, with the exception of my dog, Vida, it was difficult to make real friends. It felt lonely at times. When you make a mark in modeling, people aren't always happy for you. It can be a competitive, insecure business. More than once I'd arrive at a show to find that they'd exchanged my shoes for a much bigger size, or a few times my heel broke in the middle of the runway, forcing me to walk on tiptoes, or my sandal straps would snap—but I'd smile and just keep walking down the runway as best I could, no matter what was thrown at me. The heels models wear on runways or during photo shoots are seven or eight inches tall and walking in them is a real challenge. I'll bet every model out there has some kind of back problem. I know I do. Aside from my chronically dislocated shoulder, I have scoliosis and major issues with my knees that became worse after spending hours not only walking back and forth trying my best to balance in impossibly high heels but also contorting my body during endless photo shoots, barely breathing while holding one unnatural position after the next and trying to look at ease. It's just not normal to spend ten hours or more a day, day after day, in heels that high, and even less normal to jump in them. Because I was *always* jumping in photos; some photographers would jokingly call me Sporty Spice! The reason why is simple: I had a lot of reservations about the way I looked. I didn't feel pretty at all. The one thing I felt I could do, the one thing that gave me confidence, was *moving*. If I was in motion in a photo, springing to life and creating some kind of movement or energy, I had more tools to fill out the story the photographer wanted to tell. But in truth it was also a way of deflecting attention from my face.

I didn't confront the toll all this was taking until my panic attacks started. I experienced the first in 2003. They would last for the next nine months.

It started with a plane ride in a small, cramped six-seater. I was flying with my friends at the time to Costa Rica. The weather that day was touch-and-go, and when the plane rose in the air it began wobbling and shaking like a little leaf. *I'm going to die*, I told myself. I flew all the time and didn't think anything of it, but suddenly I was intensely aware that I had no control. The fear of being trapped in a tiny space, of not being in charge, the overwhelming feeling that nothing in the world was steady or stable. Even though my friends were trying to distract me, I felt like I was going to pass out. When we landed, I could feel something had changed in me. I don't even remember what I did that weekend. All I remember is how frightened I was to take the plane home on Sunday.

When I got back to New York, this new fear found other ways to show itself. It was as if it were moving from place to place, thing to thing, room to room. Suddenly I didn't feel right about getting on elevators. I felt I couldn't breathe. I took the stairs instead. I felt the same way about tunnels: *no way*. I'd begun traveling again for work, but now I didn't want to go inside the hotels where I was staying. Walking through windowless lobbies made it too hard to breathe. I wouldn't get on the elevator, and I didn't want to be trapped in a hotel room, especially one with windows that didn't open. I couldn't go inside a modeling studio if it had no windows. Subways were out of the question. I began walking or, if I was in New York, riding my bike or taking taxis. The goal was to avoid being shut in and trapped. Looking back, it was more likely I was trying to outrun my own anxiety.

As things got worse, I made an appointment with a specialist and then another. Both were top physicians in New York. I left one office with a high-tech machine that tracked my breath. I was told to take

Biking around New York with my guardian angel, New York, 2003.

it with me whenever I flew, sticking my finger inside as I breathed in and out while a wavy line rose and fell on a screen. It kept me from hyperventilating and getting the sweats, and it also served as a distraction. I brought the machine with me on every flight. But I didn't feel much changed. The same symptoms appeared every time. My hands would start sweating, followed by the familiar wet prickling sensation on my forehead. The back of my neck would get damp, then my hair. My breath started catching. I would feel light-headed. Sometimes I would almost faint.

Finally, things came to a crisis point. It was the weekend, and I was in my apartment in New York. I'd booked a massage to help me relax, aware that the muscles in my body were growing more tense every day. By now my panic attacks—that's what my doctors were calling them—had been going on for nearly six months. At the time I was living on West Eleventh Street and the West Side Highway, overlooking the river. My apartment was on the ninth floor. It was small but airy and full of light, with lots of windows and a big deck outside. But suddenly in the middle of my massage, I just couldn't be there anymore. I couldn't catch my own breath. Making some excuse, I got up, pulled my towel around myself, and went outside onto the deck. It was a beautiful night. There was the water and the lights in the distance, and as much air as I needed, but I still couldn't find my breath. It felt like everything in my life was going to kill me. First it was airplanes, then elevators. Then it was tunnels and hotels and modeling studios and cars. Now it was my own apartment. Everything had become a cage, and I was the animal trapped inside, panting for air. I couldn't see a way out, and I couldn't stand another day of feeling this way. The idea swept over me then: *Maybe it will be easier if I just jump. It will be all over. There's a solution. I can get out of this.*

When I think back on that moment, and that twenty-three-year-old girl, I want to cry. She is so young it almost breaks my heart. I want to tell her that everything will be all right—that she is too young to have any perspective or self-awareness, that she hasn't even begun to live her life. Up to that point I'd always thought of myself as a happy, strong, positive, confident person. I wasn't born having panic attacks. I genuinely appreciated every blessing in my life. On the outside, it seemed like I had everything! I had the largest contract in fashion with Victoria's Secret. I had wonderful parents and sisters. I loved my boyfriend. I had great friends in New York who were my family away from home. But in that moment, the only answer seemed to be to jump. It is terrifying to see how suddenly despair can take over a brain and hijack it, just like that.

Somehow I made it back inside my apartment. The idea of jumping was replaced by another thought, this one shaky but firm: *Okay, Gise, that's it. Now listen.*

Listen to yourself.

Knowing I was in even worse trouble now, I went to my doctor first thing the next morning and told him what had happened. After grilling me to make sure I wasn't still suicidal, his response was to write me a prescription for Xanax. He gave me a sample pill to hold me over while I waited to fill my prescription at the drugstore. I remember staring at the pill in his hand. In spite of how defenseless I was feeling, I thought, *I don't want to be dependent on a pill. I don't want to be dependent on anything outside myself.* The idea made me even *more* anxious. *What if I lose the pill? Then what happens?*

Something inside me knew somehow that I couldn't just put a Band-Aid over what was wrong with me. I have nothing against medicine, but when he offered me that pill, every cell in my body rose up in protest. I thought about my mother. She always looked for natural alternatives to cure any and all of our ailments when my sisters and I were growing up. She used to make teas for our sore throats or colds, and put cold towels on our foreheads and necks when one of us had a fever. Her methods had always worked, too—so what kind of tea could I make for this? I had seen people who had started off with just one pill and in time started taking many more. I was scared and didn't want to go down that path. I knew there had to be another way. I had to figure it out, since after all I'd always been the kind of person who wanted to *master* my fears.

I had a choice to make, but it was also clear I couldn't go on feeling this anxious all the time. Somehow, although I didn't know how, I knew I had to find another way. When I left the doctor's office, I threw the medication in the trash. Some things you just know are true for yourself—or your body tells you. I don't know *how* your body knows those things, but it does. Having said that for myself, I acknowledge that we are all different, with different needs. For me, I knew I needed to trust my own intuition, and handle my anxiety in the way I was most comfortable. I continue to follow my inner voice, and always encourage every person to listen to their own.

So I prayed. I prayed for clarity and for guidance about what I should do next. I asked to be shown the way. I did what I always do when I pray—I ask the same question over and over again until an answer appears. That night, I got my answer: *yoga*. At the time I wasn't looking for a *thing*. As I said, all I'd asked for was to be shown the way.

Yoga. Where did *yoga* come from? I couldn't explain it. I still can't. I knew a little bit about yoga, of course. Years earlier I'd read *Autobiography of a Yogi* by Yogananda, so it wasn't as though yoga was a foreign concept. Keep in mind this was before yoga became mainstream like it is today. Still, I had no connection to that world. How could it possibly help me? But I must have associated yoga with peace or ease or balance. So the next morning I started to look for an instructor. I also went online and began reading everything I could about yoga. Not just about the postures, but about the underlying philosophy. Yoga, I discovered, was a lot more than physical movements. It is a philosophy, a spiritual discipline that focuses on helping you know yourself better. *Yoga* comes from the Sanskrit word *yuj*, meaning to yoke, or bind. Maybe it could help me yoke together my body and mind? Maybe it could help me with my panic attacks? I read more about the breathing techniques—pranayama especially—and about meditation. *Meditation*, like yoga, back then it was just a word floating around in the culture. I'd never meditated in my life. Who had time? I was too busy. Even if you had the time, why would you bother?

When I first met Amy, my new yoga instructor, she emanated a strong sense of serenity and trustworthiness as she walked into my apartment. First, we rearranged a few pieces of furniture and then we sat on the floor using a mat. I told Amy that I had trouble breathing, and that I was afraid to get on my own elevator, so I walked nine flights of stairs instead, and that I was really scared that I was going to die. Amy started telling me about pranayama breathing. She asked me to press one finger against the middle of my forehead and use my thumb to seal my right nostril. Breathe in, she said. Now breathe out through your left. Now do it with your left nostril. Breathe in. Now breathe out through your right. She explained that the purpose of alternate-nostril breathing, as it's known, is to balance the left and right sides of the brain, which helps you relax and get centered. She then showed me a few yoga postures.

Even after only one meeting with Amy, I felt a difference. I wasn't so on edge anymore. It wasn't a miracle cure—I was still in pretty bad shape, and I had a long way to go—but Amy and I set up another meeting the next morning, and the next, and the next. I can't credit yoga entirely with the changes that took place in my life, but it helped a lot. It is still central to the life I lead today.

As I said earlier, I've always liked to dig deeply into subjects that interest me, and the more I learned about yoga, the more pranayama breathing felt important for my healing. *Prana* is the universal life-force. It's what distinguishes the living from the dead. It can be found in good-quality foods, correct breathing, and positive thinking. Pranayama breathing just means controlling the universal life-force through your breath, which in time helps bring balance and harmony to the body, the mind, and the spirit, or at least that's the goal.

Many people in the West think of yoga as physical—a form of exercise focused around asanas or postures. In fact, the entire purpose behind practicing asanas is to stretch and open up our bodies to prepare them for meditation. With Amy as my teacher, I began practicing hatha yoga, the practice of physical postures, though over the years I've also experimented with Ashtanga, kundalini, and other yogas. I love them all, but I always come back to hatha yoga because that's where I started, and it's so serene that I can be in a state of meditation while practicing. Plus a gentle practice works best for me since I do everything else in my life with intensity.

But I'm getting ahead of myself. With Amy as my teacher, I began doing alternate-nostril breathing every morning right as the sun was coming up. It got easier with practice. Meditation helps to cultivate the feeling of being present. *Presents* means gifts, and for me *presence* was the most amazing gift I could have received.

Sometimes people ask me what role yoga plays in my life today. The simple answer is that, for me, yoga, like meditation, helps me to remain present. When I get off a long plane ride I may do a few simple sun salutations or hip-openers. If I'm in Costa Rica and have the morning free, I like to do yoga with my friend Cris. I just love the exchange of energy that comes from practicing with another person. If I'm in the car and someone else is driving, I'll do my pranayama breathing in the backseat on the way to a studio, or while I'm listening to chants from devotional singers like Snatam Kaur or Krishna Das, whose voices I listened to during both my pregnancies and the births of my children. Yoga can be helpful in so many ways. Whether it involves music or mantras or breath work or meditation, it is a powerful and beautiful spiritual practice. Yoga gave me back my life.

It also motivated me to start looking inward. I decided to look closely—for the first time—at my life, to examine what was really going on with me and what role I was playing. How had I even reached this point? Why, with so many good things taking place in my life, at least on the surface, was so much else going wrong? Over the years, I've come to believe in the importance of positive attitudes. I believe that the quality of our life is directly linked to our attitudes. When my anxiety attacks started happening, people who knew me felt sorry for me. It would have been easy to buy into that way of thinking: *Why is this happening to me? Poor me! Why am I having anxiety attacks? I'm such a good person!* But if I did that, I would have seen myself as a victim. And I've always believed that when you start seeing yourself as a victim, you surrender your power, and it can be hard to get it back. From the practice of yoga and meditation, I was able to see things from a different perspective. I began to ask myself: *Gisele, why is this situation happening for you?*

There's an opportunity here—what can you learn from this? What is the lesson here?

In no way do I mean to say that if you are experiencing anxiety or depression that you should not ask for help—I did. I also know now that the early twenties are an especially vulnerable time of life. Adolescence is difficult—but your twenties, when you're still discovering who you are, and what you're good at, and where your life is going, can be even harder. Young women and men can find themselves experiencing distress they've never experienced before, and they can't understand why. If that is you, get help! It can save your life. But I didn't know that then. I'd been in charge of myself since I was fourteen, and as far as I was concerned, there was only one person who could rescue me: *me.* I learned that the only way I could begin that rescue mission was by changing the conversation inside my head.

When I began wondering, *Why is this happening to me?* a big shift in my thinking got under way. Over the next few days and weeks I began to see myself and my life more clearly. As I started to improve, I asked myself another question: *How am I going to deal with this opportunity that life has given me to learn about myself?*

Around that time I remember having the strangest feeling: I was falling away from myself and from my ego, as if they were a pair of structures toppling slowly into the surf. Life was showing me something, and its message couldn't have been clearer. It was up to me now whether I wanted to "see" what life was showing me or to hop back on the hamster wheel. It felt like I was being called on to reject everything that wasn't supporting or benefiting me and to embrace everything that was.

For example, I told myself that if I was having trouble breathing, it might be a good idea to stop smoking. I'd started when I was seventeen, sweet cigarettes at first, though pretty soon I was hooked on the regular ones. Up to a pack a day. Whenever I wanted to fit in somewhere or try to look cool, I'd light one up. I'd tried quitting a couple of times, made bets with friends, seen an acupuncturist, and read books about stopping, but with no success. Now I told myself the cigarettes had to go. So I stopped. Just like that. I began running, too, thirty minutes every morning, even when it was raining or snowing. It was partly to help with not smoking, but mostly to form a healthier habit. Nothing makes you feel your lungs more than a good hard run.

My new focus on breathing opened me up to new ways of thinking about my other habits and routines, especially my habit of always being "on the go." Traveling. Pursuing. Answering phone calls and texts and emails. Working all night and every weekend. Feeling guilty if I took even one day off. Telling myself, *You have to take this opportunity while it's here. You can rest later.* In that culture's "belief system," everything has to lead to something else—money, possessions, getting ahead in the world. Yoga, by contrast, is about *being* rather than *doing.* It's about being here right now, in *this* moment. Through yoga we learn we're already everything we need to be.

Over the next few days and weeks it became clear to me how much of my life I'd never taken the time, or given myself the space, to think about. It never occurred to me, for example, that caffeine was an upper, or that cigarettes were stimulants, or that alcohol was a depressant, or that eating junk food and candy every day could affect my body and mood. All I knew was that when I smoked, it was the only time I allowed myself to inhale and exhale fully and deeply. I thought back on all the times I'd been at parties and, feeling hemmed in, on edge, or fidgety, gone downstairs or outside to smoke.

Whatever the reason, I told myself I needed a breather. It was true: I *did* need a breather. Otherwise known as *breathing*.

Our body is a temple, but it's also a vehicle. It's a transportation device. It's no different from a car or a bike. It has only one passenger in it: the soul. That's *you*. That's *me*. And at age twenty-three, the vehicle—"my body"—that held together my soul—*me*—was breaking down. As the person responsible for creating that breakdown, I was also the only one who could fix it. It's easy to say in hindsight, but if you don't take care of your body when you're young, I guarantee you'll pay the price someday, if not in your early twenties, as I did, then in your forties or fifties.

The changes I set about making in my life came from listening deeply and trusting in myself that there had to be other alternatives. When I began practicing pranayama breathing, I felt like I was entering a new room. Once inside that room, I saw there were other rooms that needed my attention, too. Like the way I ate.

I wasn't raised to be a very healthy eater. After all, I grew up in a small Brazilian village, and my sisters and I ate what everyone else did—rice and beans with some sort of meat or vegetables. I liked snacking on the chips you could get in the supermarket, and my mother allowed all of us to drink soda on the weekends. I wolfed down Frosted Flakes with milk after volleyball practice. Around the time I quit smoking, I met Dr. Dominique, who told me my adrenal glands had completely burned out. (Whenever I visited his office, in fact, he addressed me as "Miss Adrenaline.") His theory was that my high levels of stress had caused my adrenal glands to send out too much or too little cortisol, the body's stress hormone. He made it clear my diet was harming me and advised me to give up all sugar for the next three months. Not just sugar from the wine I was drinking every night but sugar from fruit and from the carbohydrates my body broke down after I ate rice or pasta or bread. Even though I'd always loved chocolate and my morning mocha Frappuccino with whipped cream, I was disciplined—and scared—enough to do as he said.

Cutting out sugar was incredibly difficult. For the first two weeks I suffered from terrible headaches, though whether it was from doing without sugar or caffeine, or a combination, I can't say. Once my headaches went away, my entire relationship with what I ate was transformed. Was the food I was eating undermining me or supporting me? Was it taking away or giving me energy? Once I began changing my diet, it was impossible to go back. I eliminated fried food and fast food and began eating a lot more vegetables, while also experimenting with raw (uncooked) foods. I went from eating meat twice a day to twice a week. It didn't take me long to feel the difference in my energy level and, most of all, my mood. (I go into this more in chapter 7.)

There were other things I needed to get rid of, too, I realized—certain relationships weren't the best for me. Both personal and professional. Sitting in silence I asked myself, *Are these relationships good for me? Are they nourishing me?* I've always believed relationships should be based on love, respect, and trust. I thought about the relationship I was in with my boyfriend at the time. Going through so much turmoil was forcing me to ask deeper questions of myself, and when the person you love isn't asking those same questions of *himself*—and why should he have to?—you start to wonder just how much the two of you have in common. No longer numbing myself with smoking, drinking alcohol, and too much work, I was becoming more and more aware of things that I'd chosen not to look at. Was I alone in wanting to do some serious soul-searching while he stayed the same? In the end, unfortunately, the answer was yes. Not to mention that I was devoting pretty much all my energy to changing my *own* life. It wasn't my fault or his; we were just in two very different periods of our lives. A wise friend of mine once told me something I've never forgotten. *Gisele*, he said, *you have to give people the dignity of their own process.* I think about those words a lot. At the same time, it was my choice whether or not to keep someone in my life. The decision didn't mean I didn't love that person either. It meant only that I needed to love myself first and surround myself with only those things that would nourish me and those people whom I could trust.

Two or three weeks into my new regime, I began feeling calmer and more centered, more in control. My mind was no longer racing. A month later, I stood in front of the elevator in my building. *I am going to get on this thing,* I told myself. I did. My hands didn't sweat. I wasn't counting off the seconds until I reached the ninth floor. I still had to travel for work. But I no longer needed to lug a machine with me on my flights. Instead I thought, *I'm on an airplane. During the flight I'm going to read a book and maybe watch a movie.* I was still working, but mostly in contracts I needed to fulfill. I had told my agent I really needed to cut back. People might get upset or might not want to work with me again, but I told myself my well-being was more important. If I didn't have my health, or my sanity, I wouldn't have a career—or, for that matter, a life.

After three months of this new regime—yoga and pranayama breathing every morning at sunrise, meditation, exercise, no sugar, and a healthy diet—the panic attacks went away. Sometimes you need to touch rock bottom before realizing how far you have fallen. A warning sign shows up sometimes as a pinch, other times as a

My sister Fafi took this photo of Vivi and me in Paris in 2013, doing yoga in the early a.m. before going to work.

punch. We are always getting messages during the day and when we sleep. We can either listen to them and do something about them, or we can block them out. But this experience taught me that if you don't listen to those messages, the louder and more intense they'll get. You'll end up either with an epiphany or with some kind of destruction. Thank God, for me it wasn't the latter.

Even though that was a very challenging time, it really brought home how it's my choice to see life either positively or negatively. The first breath we take when we enter our body as newborns we take by ourselves. So is our last. Between those two breaths, we have some important decisions to make. We can't choose the circumstances of our lives, but we *can* choose how we experience them. At the end of our lives, do we want to think back on our own bad attitudes and behavior? The moments we acted out of cruelty, or jealousy, or fear, or said something unkind to someone else? Do we want to walk through life weighed down with our pockets full of heavy stones?

For as long as I can remember, my desire has always been to live in harmony, as lightly and with as few regrets as possible. I'll give an example. If I become angry at someone, and don't let it go, but keep thinking about it, the anger can consume me. In fact it will consume me. The only person who can get rid of that anger is me. Why? Because I was the one responsible for creating that anger—which means I'm also the one who's in charge of getting rid of it. First, though, I need to accept what I'm feeling and why. I need to be completely honest with myself. Is there a real injustice here I need to address, or is this some petty issue I should let go? Is someone else being hurt, or is this anger just hurting me? Only with an openness to learn, accept, and be honest can I ever hope to change. If I don't acknowledge my anger, I become like a dog locked in the basement who bares his teeth whenever the door opens.

Writing in my journal during a yoga retreat, Sedona, Arizona, 2014.

That's why whenever I feel weighted down by anger or fear, the first thing I do is accept my feelings. I see the turmoil as a visitor just passing through. Then, consciously, I say goodbye to it, knowing I was the one who allowed it to come in the first place. I don't let go of those feelings because I'm an amazingly unselfish person either! I let go because in the end it's better for me. The only person living inside my brain, body, and soul is me. No one else is responsible for what I'm feeling. But this also means I'm the only one who can resolve the emotional upheaval.

To my mind, there is nothing worse than reaching the end of your life and knowing you are responsible for hatred or division. I've heard it said that we're born with the faces God gave us but we end up with the faces we deserve. At the end of my life, the only thing that will matter to me is whether or not I was a good person. A loving person. An addition to this life—not a subtraction. Someone who experienced life fully, who lived her truth, who loved life, and the earth, and

The family that does tree pose together . . . well, you can probably figure out the rest. That's Tom holding Vivi, with me, Benny, and Jack in front, Bahamas, 2014.

had a positive impact on the world. I hope my own face someday reflects all of these intentions. My dad used to tell me that at the end of the day, when I put my head on my pillow, I needed to be able to live with every choice I made so I could sleep through the night and wake up in the morning feeling good about myself.

When I think of love I always think about my family. In 2003, as I was making one change in my life after another, my family became my focus. Living between New York and LA, and traveling all the time, I realized how much I missed my parents and my sisters and how being on the hamster wheel hadn't just disconnected me from myself; it had also disconnected me from them. When you go through a crisis, or a period when you don't feel safe, you want to be near the people whose love and support are constant. Our families are our harbors, our safe spaces. No family is perfect, but I believe my family always has my back. When I'm around my parents and sisters, I have no defenses. They accept me as I am, both the shadows *and* the light, and I do the same with them. We speak a common language. If my sisters and I are talking, and one of us starts crying, a few seconds later we're *all* crying. *Always.* If one of them asks, "Why are you crying?" the answer is always, "I'm crying because *you're* crying!"

Love is the best therapy. Cuddling with my friend's cat during a trip with my parents to South Africa when I was working on healing from my panic attacks, Cape Town, 2003.

That's why later that year I went home to Horizontina. I wanted to be around people who spoke my language, especially since I hadn't spent much time with my family since I'd left to begin my career. I felt like I was fourteen years old all over again. I drank my mom's special teas. I helped out with the clothes washing and the house-cleaning. At night I helped make empanadas in the kitchen, just as I'd done when I was little. I spent as much time as I could with my five sisters, and that year we even went to Bahia for Carnival together. Slowly I got stronger. Steadier. Happier. I felt more and more at home. At home with myself. At home with the people I loved most, who loved me back.

Most people can't and shouldn't go it alone. Asking for help is never a sign of failure but a show of strength and confidence, and knowing your life is worth saving. At the same time, I'm also convinced that none of us learn, or grow, from the easy times in our lives. If my panic attacks hadn't happened, I would never have felt the need to change. Not physically. Not mentally. Not spiritually. The difficulties that came so close to killing me was, in the end, what gave me a whole new life. The most negative period I'd ever experienced became the most transformative, and the greatest blessing. In many respects, that twenty-three-year-old girl *did* die. But when she came back, she was much happier and healthier. She had learned about suffering and the many gifts it offers, as well as how the darkest times in our lives can be our greatest teachers.

3

The Quality of Your Life Depends on the Quality of Your Relationships

ise, my father said to me one day, during our seven-hour drive from the airport in Porto Alegre to our home in Horizontina, *at the end of your life, what will you remember? The house you lived in? The car you drove? The magazine covers you were on?* He didn't wait for an answer. *No,* he said. *The quality of your life depends on the quality of your relationships.*

My dad and I had a lot of meaningful conversations during the long drives to and from the airport, especially when I was visiting home between the ages of fourteen and fifteen. I would always leave Horizontina with good advice from my father. I often think about what my dad said about relationships. The quality of my life really *does* depend on the quality of my relationships. The memories of my interactions with the people I love stays with me longer than other experiences. The talks I had with my son before bed. The conversations with my daughter on the drive to school. The moments shared

I loved my conversations with my dad when he picked me up at the airport. I took this photo of him behind the wheel.

with a partner or a friend over dinner. Imagine how unhappy our lives would be if we spent all our time alone, with no one around us, no one to count on or share our experiences. That's why the biggest blessings in my life are my husband, my children, my parents, my sisters, my friends, my pets (yes, my pets are my companions too)—who accompany me through my life. Most people probably think that when they leave school they say goodbye to their teachers. But really, all our relationships are teaching us about ourselves one way or another. Because each relationship allows us to see different aspects of ourselves.

In the end, the longest and most important relationship any of us will ever have is with ourselves. That's why I believe self-awareness is so important. We all need to learn to become comfortable with ourselves as early as possible, and to grasp that we are responsible for who we are. And, as I said, the best way to get to know ourselves is through our relationships with others. Relationships may be casual or based on friendship. They may develop from work-related activities, or be romantic. Some are short-term. Others can last a lifetime. Relationships can vary tremendously. Some examples: I've been in a friendship that urged me to make positive changes, but then the other person's behavior was stagnant and didn't grow—or sometimes it's been the other way around, when I have been the one who was afraid to change. With other relationships, I've come to the realization that the only thing we had in common was a time in our lives that is now in the past. Friends move, or change jobs, or get married, or get divorced. However, what is consistent is that all our relationships are important for our growth.

A good way to start to figure out who you are is to examine how you treat yourself and others. In my early twenties, I was extremely hard on myself. I was working in a business where girls (that's what they always called us, too—"girls") are judged every day by how they look. I turned that same critical eye on myself. Plus the criticisms I'd heard back in school and when I started modeling—*your nose is too big, your eyes are too small*—were stuck in my head like a broken record. So often the work I was doing didn't satisfy me. The angle was wrong. The lighting was wrong. *I* was wrong. Obviously, being so self-critical didn't feel very good. Being judgmental the way I was back then, and taking personally other people's negative projections, is really destructive.

Only after I began meditating and practicing yoga did I set off on the long road of becoming more compassionate toward myself. People who begin a meditation practice often first notice a judgmental voice inside their own head. Self-criticism. Even paranoia. *Why did I say that? Why didn't I deal with that situation differently?* Inside my twenty-something brain was a movie camera that kept playing the same disapproving films over and over again. The same spool, the same loop, the same characters, the same dialogue. Of all the many lessons meditation has taught me, the most important has been about the power of my own thoughts to help or harm me.

I've always had very high standards for myself—and have expected that the people around me would share that commitment. But over the years I've learned that this is not necessarily the case. Everyone has their own timing and way of doing things. With this realization came another: that everyone, me included, is going through something no one else knows, everyone has a story—and therefore it's important to remember to be kind to ourselves and to everyone we meet.

I still have moments when I push myself too hard. The difference is that I'm now aware of my imbalances. When I have thoughts that really don't serve me, I now see them as visitors or walk-on characters in a movie. I just observe them—it feels very much like being seated in the back row of a theater—giving me the objectivity to say to myself, "Oh, you're thinking about that again!" and then I breathe those nasty thoughts away. By refocusing on my breath, I make a conscious effort to change the conversation in my head. I do this over and over again, every single time I meditate, and throughout my day. (Once, in the middle of my morning meditation, when Benny was quite small, the thought crossed my mind that I hadn't cut up the grapes that I had put in his school lunch box. I was seized by the thought that he would choke on an uncut grape! I nearly lost it—and had to talk myself out of it and focus more deeply until I could see that my fear was talking, not my clarity. Then I was fine. Meditation helps me to stay calm and clear—even when it involves grapes.)

When I first came to New York at age sixteen, it was a big transition for me in so many ways. The first was cultural. As a Brazilian, I would greet almost everyone with a hug and a kiss. That's what I knew! Brazilians are warm and demonstrative. Two minutes after you meet a Brazilian, she's inviting you over to her house for dinner and you're calling her "Auntie." Americans aren't always that way. In my early New York days, people would freeze, or pull away from me, or just stand there looking confused. *Don't they like me?* I wondered. *Did I just do something wrong?*

This is one small example of how important it is not to be hurt or confused by our diversity. We shouldn't expect others to be like us.

Left to right: With my longtime agent, Anne, and my mom, New York City, 2000. I was probably twenty in this photo.

When I reflect on my teens and twenties, those years consisted of hundreds of conversations that took place inside my own head. Even when many conversations involved other people I was still in a constant run-on dialogue with myself.

Who am I? was the most common one. *Am I who other people think I am? If not, am I hiding who I really am? Am I drinking too much? What's my limit? Should I stop smoking?* There were others, too: *Am I someone who needs to spend time alone? Do I like going to parties, or do I feel more comfortable around a small group of friends? What sorts of romantic relationships work best for me?* This type of questioning, I'm guessing, takes place inside all our heads, to help us figure out our likes and dislikes, our limits, our routines, and what makes us feel good or feel bad, not to mention what we want out of life. Through asking ourselves fundamental questions we come to terms with our priorities and values.

Having said this, learning about yourself through being involved with other people is completely different from comparing yourself with other people. It may sound hard to believe, but I go out of my way not to compare myself with anyone. I've been *inspired* by other people, but that doesn't mean I've measured myself against them. Comparing yourself with another person is pointless. Why? Because all of us have something special to offer since each one of us is unique. If you spend time comparing yourself with someone else, the only thing you're doing is setting yourself up for disappointment and failure. You won't *ever* feel good enough. There are seven and half billion people in the world, so chances are that someone will always be "better" than you in some respect. But is that person *you*? Did she grow up in your family? Did she grow up at the same time you did, share your parents, your siblings, your childhood, your teachers, your friends, your advantages, your disadvantages, your education, your jobs, or . . . ? Of course she didn't. When we frame things that way, the idea of comparing ourselves to other people seems ridiculous. I compare myself with only one person: *me*. Am I doing the best I can at my job? Am I being the best wife, the best mother, the best friend, the best human being? How can I keep learning and improving?

I've always been a receptive, porous person, attuned to the energy other people give off. That's one reason why over the years I've learned to be more selective with my friendships. In my teens and twenties, I wanted to be friends with *everyone*! I also considered it my job, even my responsibility, to protect them. Basically I was invested in making sure everyone around me was happy. I'd been that way since I was young. If Pati and Gabi got into a fight, they always came crying to me, and I'd be the referee and peacemaker. I was always bringing home cats and dogs I found abandoned on the streets, and if Raque wasn't paying attention to her pet bunny, I took it upon myself to care for it. When I started making friends in New York in my teens, I quickly became known as a good "psychotherapist." So many people were telling me their problems that at one point my sister Fafi joked that I should start charging an hourly fee!

I wanted only the best for the people in my life, and assumed this feeling would be mutual. Unfortunately, I learned the hard way that this wasn't always the case. When I first began making money, I was happy to give it away to anyone who needed some. Having grown up sharing a bedroom with three sisters and dividing up a single chocolate bar into six equal pieces, sharing was all I knew. You don't have any money to pay rent? Here, let me help you with that! Having problems with your boyfriend? Then use my apartment! You don't have anything to wear? Take my dress, take my shoes! Well, it didn't take long for my naïveté to get whipped out of me. At one point I realized that no matter how much I gave, it never seemed to be enough. In fact, some people got so used to my generosity that they would get upset when I said, *Sorry, this time I can't help you.* I was left feeling hurt and used. I learned that in any relationship, no way should one person do all the giving, and the other person all the taking, because resentment will start building up from both sides and the friendship will become damaged. Kabballah, which is a philosophy I studied for a while, has a concept known as "Bread of Shame." It says that people need to do the work of Transformation in order to earn the Light. If we are over-giving or doing something for a person that they have not earned, we are giving them Bread of Shame. If we take more than we give, then we are consuming Bread of Shame. Sometimes the best way to be loving is to give other people the space to earn the Light for themselves. After getting burned a number of times, I started to choose more carefully the people I kept close to me. Along the way I learned another significant lesson: if you're a person who gives and gives—of your money, your apartment, your car, your clothes, your time, and your love—sometimes you're the one who is out of balance. A wise older friend once told me, "You need to give people the opportunity to do what they can and must do for themselves." We all go through whatever it is we need to go through in order to evolve and grow, and you don't want to get in the way of that process.

I recently had a talk with a good friend who has always been an over-giver. He was having some personal issues and this time needed my help. When it was time to go, he thanked me over and over again. "Look," I said, "you're the one who goes around giving and helping—and in the past you've helped me. Sometimes it's important to give others the opportunity to help you. If you're always the one who's doing the giving, well, it's actually kind of selfish." It is a lesson I wish I'd learned earlier. The truth is that asking other people for help is not a sign of weakness, but actually gives them an opportunity to feel empowered. I was happy that my friend let me give back to him, because reciprocating in my relationships makes *me* feel good.

These days I'm probably not as immediately warm and open as I once was (though I'm still Brazilian). But I still choose to believe that people are good at heart and I often focus beyond their personality on the spiritual essence that is animating them. The spirit is the beautiful spark of goodness that resides in everyone. In particular I enjoy being around people who inspire me and bring out my best. People who are kind, intelligent, and compassionate. I also don't like beating around the bush. Be direct—I can take it. I hope I give back these same qualities to my friends. Time is the biggest gift any of us is given, and we all have a limited amount of it. The biggest gift we can give anyone is just that—our *time,* our *love.*

We may be able to choose our friends, but we can't choose our families—which makes our parents and siblings our first and greatest teachers. (Certainly they're the most influential.) I've always been extremely close to my family, and few relationships mean more to me than the ones I have with my five sisters. Raque, Fofa, Pati, Gabi, and Fafi—I know, it's a mouthful—comfort me, challenge me, and protect me. They bring stability to my life. My family always gets me, and I don't have my walls up around them. I can't! They would see right through them. My parents and sisters know me better than anyone and they are constantly providing me with feedback, whether I like it or not.

As the oldest, Raque, who was only seven when my twin sister, Pati, and I were born, is basically my second mother. (There is a fourteen-year age difference between Raque and our youngest sister, Fafi.) When Pati and I arrived, my mother made a wise move. She told Raque and also Fofa (who's two years younger than Raque) that they could each choose a baby to care for and help feed and diaper. That baby would be her responsibility. Working as hard as my mom did as a teller at Banco do Brasil, and with so many girls in the house, she needed to find as many helpers as possible. Raque may have been my second mother, but she is also my older sister, and she loved to tease us for fun—because what older sibling hasn't done that? Our grandma lived five hours away in the country and, as I said before, she did everything, including raising and slaughtering her own chickens. Whenever there was a chicken head lying around, Raque enjoyed taking it and racing after my sisters and me. We would run and lock ourselves in the bathroom trying to escape. Another time when I was young, we went to visit my grandparents' graveyard, which was separated by a fence beside a field with a grazing cow. There were a bunch of plastic flowers on the ground, so I placed a few on the wooden fence to decorate it and try to cheer things up. The next time we went back there, the plastic flowers and the cow were gone. Raque told me the cow had choked on the plastic flowers I had left on the fence, and died. For days I felt terrible, but then again, who doesn't love having an older sibling with such a great sense of humor?!

I love Raque more than anything, and she has my lifelong gratitude. She always took great care of all of us ever since we were born, and as the eldest girl, she's also our family's official memory keeper. If my mom doesn't remember something that happened when we were little, Raque is always there to fill in the blanks.

Graziela, the second eldest—we all call her Fofa—was always an overachiever. She was the first to leave home, to study at a top-quality high school located in Brasilia, where our grandparents lived. So she moved there. My parents wanted to give their daughters the best possible education. After attending an excellent high school and graduating with two degrees at the same time from the Federal University, Fofa was qualified to be a federal public servant. Later, at age twenty-six, she became a federal judge. She's probably the fairest, most rational, and analytical of all of us, as well as a beautiful, selfless person. (Her nickname in our family is Mother Teresa.) She's also an incredible chef, and loves having the whole family over to try out her delicious recipes.

As a twin, I always used to wonder, *Where do I begin, and where does Pati begin? Are she and I the same person, two parts of the same person, or separate people entirely?* Having a twin sister is like growing up with your own personal measuring stick or thermometer. That became even clearer to me when Pati at age ten was diagnosed with double pneumonia, and the doctors weren't sure if she would live. I was traumatized. The thought of Pati being close to death was so terrible that I couldn't even fully grasp it. She was in intensive care for almost a month, but to me it felt like an eternity. For the first week I wasn't even allowed to see her. When I finally visited, she couldn't even talk. She was stuck there with oxygen tubes to help her breathe. I kept asking when she was coming home, but my mom said she couldn't tell. My twin sister had been by my side my whole life, and all of a sudden she wasn't. I was devastated. When Pati was in the hospital, I promised to pray to God every night for her to heal. Praying was the only thing that comforted me. Life seemed suddenly so fragile, as though it could break apart in a moment, just like that. When I wasn't sitting by Pati's bed in the hospital, I was at home in our bedroom, folding and refolding her shirts and pants, getting them ready for when she came home. Thank *God* she *did* come home, and from that point on I began appreciating life in new ways, with more gratitude, and with a much closer connection to spirit.

Like any siblings, Pati and I are alike in some ways, different in others. Starting when we were teenagers, for example, I was nearly a foot taller than she was. Pati was more popular and social and loved being with her friends, whereas I preferred spending time alone, climbing trees and getting lost in my own little world. I thought Pati was so cool! She also inspired me at school. She was a very good student, which inspired me to study as hard and do well.

I have always loved music and enjoy singing. In fact, Pati, Gabi, and I all sang in the school chorus. It was so much fun! There's an old saying in Portuguese that in English translates to "Who sings sends away his worries." On Sundays, we usually had *churrasco*, grilled beef, chicken, or pork on sticks cooked inside a hot fire. During *churrascos*, my dad always brought out his guitar and everyone in our family sang. I knew Pati didn't have a high opinion of her singing voice, and I remember being aware of her discomfort and never wanting her to feel bad. At the same time, playing guitar and singing with my father was one of the highlights of my week.

Gabriela, or Gabi, was and still is the funniest and the most rebellious of all of us. There was never a dull moment when she was around. Gabi is only one year younger than Pati and me, and growing up we were a trio, a Brazilian version of the Three Musketeers. If I thought I gave my teachers a hard time in school, it was nothing compared with Gabi, who was *always* getting into trouble. Before Fafi came along, Gabi spent five years as the baby of our family, and it couldn't have been easy for her to give up that role. Today Gabi is a lawyer, intelligent, funny, and intense, and possibly even harder on herself than I am on myself. She is a perfectionist and feels it is her job to "protect" everyone in our family, and in the process sometimes forgets to take care of herself. Happily today she is more aware of this and working on finding a balance.

Finally there's Fafi, *my* baby. Since Fafi was born I became *her* second mother, or, rather, one of her five second mothers. Fafi likes to joke that she's our mom's favorite, but I think she is also the favorite of *all* her second mothers, too. After Fafi turned seven, she basically grew up as an only child with the run of the house. Like all my sisters, Fafi is a smart, beautiful, loving, supportive person. Today she has become like a second mother to Benny and Vivi, and there are no words to describe my endless gratitude for her. She is also the hipster in the family. It was Fafi who told me I should go on Instagram and Facebook. At first I said no. I've never enjoyed spending much time on the internet, and I've always been very private and didn't want to display myself that way. It also sounded too high-maintenance. But Fafi persuaded me that social media was the best way to show the world who I really am, and I have to admit she had a point.

Along with Tom, my children, and my parents, I love my sisters more than anyone else in the world. The six of us spent our lives sharing, starting with our bedroom, the clothes we wore, and the chores we divided up around our house. I see the six of us as collaborators, and few things give me more joy than working with them. At one point in my life, many of my relationships—with my boyfriend, with my then-longtime agent—were either falling apart or being exposed for what they really were. Wanting me to feel I had at least *one* safe space, my father had an idea. After all, who always had my back? Who did I trust? My sisters. So when my dad suggested we all work together, it was a no-brainer. I feel so blessed that I got to grow up surrounded by six incredible women—my mon and my five sisters. Besides some hair-pulling and scratches when we were young, I have always considered my sisters my best friends, and there is nothing in the world I wouldn't do for them and I know that goes both ways.

Before long, Pati organized a company in Brazil, and one by one my sisters came on board. At first none of them had any idea what the fashion world was about, and why should they? But they took the time to learn. For the past ten years, we have all worked together, except Fofa, who is still a federal judge, though that doesn't stop her from giving her opinion any time a big decision needs to be made. I trust my sisters implicitly. We are all so different, but, as my dad says, we complement one another, help one another grow, and in general are really great together! Even when we have disagreements, or are tough with one another at times, we will always love and protect each other, no matter what. They're all incredible at what they do. We're a family, but we're also a great team. Teamwork makes the dream work.

That's not to say there aren't moments when one of us gets upset and begins hollering. Family members typically reserve their most hurtful words for one another. As I said, with family members, your walls are down. Still, if anyone isn't treating me right, whether it's a friend or one of my sisters, my response is always the same: *I am only going to be in relationships that are loving and respectful. When you are*

With all my sisters, celebrating New Year's in Los Angeles, 2000. From left to right, that's Raque, Fofa, Fafi, me, Gabi, and Pati.

ready to resume a loving, respectful relationship, I am happy to talk to you. If you're not ready yet, it's okay. I will be here when you are.

We learn a lot from our families. And then if we create a new family with a partner, then a lot more learning takes place. Especially with our children. It seems to me that everything has become raw and real and unfiltered with my children. Getting married and having kids has brought me face-to-face with an entirely new set of mirrors. I've noticed that everything that's unsettled or extreme about my own personality has a funny way of spilling onto my husband and children and reflecting back onto me!

I've always been an impatient person. (My children and my sisters have made this very clear.) Usually I have lots of ideas, projects, and interests going on at the same time. I am definitely hyperactive, but in some ways I feel that has served me well. My mind sometimes works faster than my mouth can form words, and I'm someone who likes things to be done *yesterday*. So impatience has always been a big issue for me. I'm better than I used to be, and for this I credit my children, but I still have a long way to go. By nature Benny isn't impatient, but last year I noticed he was starting to get testy. Well, since I knew this pattern of behavior wasn't coming from Tom, whose fault was that if not mine? Becoming a mother has inspired me to work on myself even more than usual because I know I'm setting the emotional tone for my family, and also acting as a mirror for my children and husband. I always remind my kids that we are all here learning, and that our learning never, ever stops.

Earlier I spoke about how our teens and twenties are a time of intense inner negotiation. And few experiences teach us more about our wants, our needs, and our expectations than romantic relationships. In the past, I've been in romances where I felt I was swimming in fast-moving waters, and others where the water was calm and still. When I chose Tom to be my life partner, I was fortunate to find a man calmer than he is stormy. As his teammates will tell you, Tom is someone you can count on. It's a quality I hadn't experienced in any of my other romantic relationships. I love my husband—and most of all, I trust him. With Tom, who provides our family with a stable foundation, I'm able to create a *home*.

We also complement each other. Our values are similar. We're both disciplined in our daily routines and habits. We're both committed to good health and good nutrition (though I'll eat a cookie if I want one, and Tom usually won't). My husband is rational, analytical, and a man of few words. I'm emotional, intuitive, changeable, and a woman of many words. I've learned a lot from Tom. When Benny was younger, he dislocated his elbow and started screaming.

I was frantic until Tom appeared and took control of the situation. I might never be as cool, calm, and collected as Tom is, but I'm working at it. I like to believe that Tom's stability and steadiness give me the space and the freedom I need to fly, and that the little bird inside me knows—and Tom likes to remind me—that she's held tightly to a slender, invisible string he keeps deep in one of his pockets.

With my family, I naturally fall into the role of nurturer. Tom works long days, and when he comes home, I want to make sure I am there for him. But from the beginning Tom trusted me enough to talk to me—

Benny and Vivi giving Daddy some love in the kitchen in Boston after a tough loss in 2016.

really talk to me—and over the years I learned to stop talking as much and started being a better listener. As my dad likes to say, *that's why we were born with only one mouth and two ears.*

Sometimes I think we can put too much pressure and responsibility on our marriages and partnerships. We expect our partners to be our lovers, our best friends, our advisers, our *everything.* This isn't to say that in the course of any relationship we don't play those roles, and that our partners don't do the same for us. But why should one partner be responsible for the sum total of the other person's experience? It's unfair and limiting to both. After all, our lives are made up of so many relationships, and we learn different things from all of them.

Every relationship has something to add to our lives, even the difficult ones. I feel that in any relationship we are either learning, or teaching, sometimes both. I love harmony, and I love living in harmony with the people around me—and I believe that nothing creates harmony better than treating others the way we want to be treated. The energy and intention you put out is what counts. By sharing love, it's more likely that you will get love back. But even when that doesn't happen, I just keep on giving love. It's who I am, and it's what makes me feel good.

To my way of thinking, there is nothing more amazing than going through life fostering meaningful relationships. How great does it feel when you can really be there for another person, and then, years later, without any expectations, that person is there for you? How incomplete would our lives be without those relationships? At the

A picture of my friends from Believe Earth, right after my speech at Rock in Rio: (*left to right*) Pati, Estela, Me, Ana Lu, Marcos, and Pedro.

end of the day, it's not about rushing to get to the destination; it's about enjoying the journey along the way, and that journey is made up of moments, experiences, and interactions with other people—and sometimes animals. *That's* what creates memories. *That's* what really matters.

Instinct also plays a part in our future relationships. After all, you never know when you'll meet the people who may end up having a positive and lasting influence in your life. I've always had good luck whenever I follow my inner voice. A few years ago, I remember hearing about a man named Pedro, who was a key figure in regenerative agriculture in Brazil. One time when I was in São Paulo, I saw Pedro's face on the cover of a magazine on the table at my hotel. I called my sister Pati to see if it was possible to arrange a meeting with him. Pati did set up a meeting, and soon my dad, Gabi, Fafi, and I went to visit Pedro at his beautiful farm, where we had a great conversation about nature and the need for all of us to work hard to protect the earth. Around this same time, I was asked to participate in a documentary film, *The Beginning of Life*, about the importance of a child's first twenty-four months of life. Knowing that the filmmaker, Estela, is passionate about education and early childhood development, I wanted to help, so of course I said yes. Over the course of subsequent meetings with Pedro, I learned that he was good friends with Ana Lu, who happened to work with Estela, and who started the Alana Institute, which is devoted to helping children thrive through quality education. Only a few months after meeting Pedro, I met Ana Lu, her husband, Marcos, and Estela, when they were in Boston. Our positive connection was instantaneous. So we made a plan to have dinner at Ana and Marcos's house the next time I would be in Brazil. When we got together, we discussed how we could unite forces to create positive change in the world. We sat in a circle outside on the grass during a beautiful full moon and shared our thoughts and beliefs about creating a better world by spreading positivity and hope.

That was the birth of Believe Earth. Our intention was to create a platform to showcase people who are making positive contributions to the world. Our mission statement is *If you believe, the future can be unbelievable.* How could I have known that Pedro, Estela, and Ana and Marcos were friends? Or that my instinct to contact Pedro and the fact that I participated in *The Beginning of Life* documentary would create the spark that led to the founding of Believe Earth? Life truly is an adventure and we never know where our friend-ships will lead us—which is what makes them so interesting.

I believe that all our relationships—including our marriages or partnerships—come to us to support our growth, and give us the op-portunity to learn to create happiness and fulfillment. All our rela-tionships together form a kind of mosaic. On mine the largest area belongs to Tom, Benny, Vivi, Jack, and our extended families. There are also parts of the mosaic of my life that belong to the friends I made during my early days in New York—Nino, Helly, Robby, Jody, Anne, Harry, Amber, Kevin, and Katie. Other pieces are reserved for child-hood friends from Horizontina and for friends I have from all over the world who have inspired me and shared my passion and purpose for making the world a better place. Others represent friendships I've made at my children's school, and friendships Tom and I created to-gether. And yet there are large sections that are still blank. It's re-served for all the friends and teachers I haven't met yet. My goal is to keep learning about myself and others until I take my last breath—to experience my life to the fullest. That's why I'm *here.*

At my baby shower with some of my closest friends, Boston, 2009.

One of the longest and most important relationships of my life wasn't with another person. It was with a dog. A beautiful, funny, playful, loving, irresistible little dog named Vida. A day doesn't pass when I don't think about her and miss her. Believe me when I say I wouldn't have accomplished very much in my job or my life without Vida.

I think of dogs as guardian angels, as protectors in animal form. Vida and I came into each other's lives when I was eighteen years old. For two years I'd been living out of a suitcase in New York City in a models' apartment—four rooms with two bunk beds apiece, a revolving crash pad for girls from all over the world—on East Thirty-Fifth Street. I was working literally every day and at night memorizing English phrases from my Mariah Carey and Boyz II Men cassettes, since I was too busy to attend my intensive English classes.

Since leaving Brazil, I'd been completely independent and in charge of my own life. Despite being an eighteen-year-old girl living almost five thousand miles away from my family, I did not think of myself as lonely. But maybe I felt more alone than I realized, because when Vida came into my life, she gave me comfort and love that I didn't even know were missing.

I first saw Vida in the front window of a store called American Kennels. I was either coming from or going to a casting when I saw the tiniest, most adorable dog I'd ever seen frolicking in a nest of straw on Madison Avenue and Sixty-Second Street. She was so small she could have easily fit in my hand. I went inside, stretched out on the floor, and played with her for the next few hours. I lost all track of time. Just seeing her in the window made me fall in love with her, spending time with her made the relationship official. She, Vida, was the one. I was sure of it. I found out she was a Teacup Yorkie, a breed I didn't know anything about. I *did* know there was no way I was leaving that store without her.

It was late afternoon, and right before closing time I handed the clerk my credit card. At three hundred dollars, the price was very high, I thought, but I reminded myself that American Kennels sold pedigreed dogs to Upper East Siders and was as far from a puppy mill as you could get. I left the store with my new best friend, tucking her under my coat to keep her warm, and she and I began our great adventure together. In that one moment my life changed. It wasn't just about me living in New York, and working all the time, and

Me with my single braid and single feather earring, and baby Vida, a few days after she and I found each other, in front of the apartment I was subletting on Tenth and University Place in New York (they had kicked us out of the models' apartment). Look how tiny Vida is! Look at that face!

memorizing Mariah Carey and Boyz II Men lyrics under my blankets. It was now Vida and me against the world!

There was only one problem: the models' apartment had a strict no-pets rule. I wasn't allowed to stay there with Vida. There was no question, I wouldn't return Vida to the store. I told the other girls that my new dog weighed only two pounds and could literally fit in my hand. Did she really count as a pet? The building rules didn't apply to someone that small, did they? Could I stay there just one more night and make a new plan in the morning? The next day, knowing I didn't have enough money to rent an apartment or stay in a hotel, I found a room in an SRO by the Midtown Tunnel—shared toilets, shared showers, a small dark room with only a bed and a sink—where I lived for the next week. It was a gloomy, scary place. When I told my agent about my new living situation, she told me she feared for my life. The next day she found me a sublet in the West Village whose owner, another model, was working in Paris for the next few months.

Vida still didn't have a name. The Brazilian word for *life* is *vida*, and I kept hugging and kissing her while saying, *Minha vida! Minha vida! My life! My life!* So she became Vida. It was the perfect name for her, too, because Vida *did* become my life. Then, a few days after I moved into my sublet, the phone rang. It was my mother, and she sounded furious. My credit card was linked to hers, and the credit card bill had just come in the mail. At the time I was getting some good exposure as a model and building my portfolio, but I wasn't making much money yet. When I did shows or appeared in magazines, I would usually walk away with around one hundred dollars. I had a little money I'd socked away from working in Japan, and my agency gave me advances they deducted from whatever jobs I got, but my mom and I still shared a joint account, since she felt I was too young to be completely in charge of my own finances. That's how she learned I'd just spent three thousand dollars at a store called American Kennel, and *Gise, do you know how much money that is, and what in heaven's name are you thinking?* I felt my whole stomach cramp up. I hadn't noticed that extra zero. If I thought three hundred dollars was a lot of money, three thousand dollars was unimaginable. I could still hear my mom's voice—she worked as a bank teller and knew the value of a dollar. But she *had* to understand. Whether it was three hundred or three thousand dollars, buying Vida was the best thing I'd ever done. *Mom,* I kept saying, *you don't understand. We're talking about Vida!*

Let me say it again, everything I accomplished in my career or life wouldn't have been possible without Vida. Vida was there for me always. She was the only constant in my life. Every day she made me happier, more joyful, and more complete. She was my angel, my shield, my bodyguard, my baby, my daughter, my mother, my closest friend. With Vida around, I was never alone. I could just be an eighteen-year-old girl.

When the model whose apartment I sublet returned home from Paris, I went on and sublet another one, this time on Fifty-Eighth and Eighth Avenue. I found it through an ad in the paper. This apartment cost six hundred dollars a month, which was all I could afford at the time. It was a cramped studio, the kitchen two black burners and a mini-fridge, the bathroom shower a hose sticking down from the ceiling. Prostitutes gathered outside every night at the end of the block. I slept on a mattress on the floor, with Vida next to me. One night I saw something moving around slowly and called out, "Vida?" But I could feel her body next to mine, and when I turned on the light, I saw a rat three times Vida's size crawling around right near me. The next morning I bought mouse traps at the supermarket. Not only was my mother scheduled to visit me soon, but people told me that rats could eat someone as small as Vida.

Vida cried a lot when she was little, so I decided to take her with me wherever I went. I had a small bag, a combination carryall and purse. When I picked up the bag, she was all ready to go. Vida would leap into it, stick out her little head, and the two of us were off and running. She was completely without fear. I think she thought she was part flying squirrel. Even if I was walking past her casually with my bag open, I'd hear a *whoosh* sound, like wings beating, and suddenly my bag would be four pounds heavier.

My mom and me in front of the apartment building where I lived for a while in 1998, the same place where one night I saw a rat that was even bigger than Vida.

Soon Vida was a familiar sight at studios and runway shows. Everyone knew Vida was my dog. She sat in my lap when I got my hair and makeup done. During runway shows, she either stayed in her bag, or I put her on a leash, since otherwise she would have gone racing down the runway after me. Vida was extremely social. She liked making the rounds and making new friends. Knowing how much distance she covered, people began using her as a messenger. Vida would show up with a yellow sticky note on her collar: *Hey, Gisele, I just gave Vida some bacon*, or *Hey, Gisele, could you please meet me in Studio 6?* One time Vida showed up backstage wearing hair extensions, and another time my dear friend the photographer Steven Meisel took a Polaroid of her with the legend *VOGUE* in the background so Vida could make her cover girl debut. More than once I spotted her in my dressing room with half a bagel hanging from her mouth. After she began swelling up like a balloon, I had to beg people not to give her treats. If for some reason I couldn't bring Vida with me to work, she was always there at home to greet me excitedly and jump onto my lap. Every night she slept beside me on my bed, or on my pillow, with her little face right next to mine. At night I felt the fast beat of her heart. It was as if the two of us were connected by an invisible cord. She was as much a part of me as I was of her.

When I wasn't working or sleeping, I was on an airplane going to

My little partner and me in my last job before Benny was born, 2009.

the next job. No matter where I went—Europe, the Far East—Vida came with me. She was a very good traveler, too, quiet and well behaved. Vida was by my side when I first met Tom, when Jack was young, and when Benny was born. When I moved to Boston, Vida immediately made it clear that she was the queen of the house and our family's chief guard dog and protector. When Benny was little, if anyone dared to enter his room when he was sleeping, Vida would snarl. Tom loved Vida, too. She was no longer a puppy by then, and whenever I had to take one- or two-day trips, Tom took her with him to Gillette Stadium so she wouldn't have to be by herself all day. Believe me, he loved it! He told me once that Vida used to chase Randy Moss, the Patriots' wide receiver, around the locker room and that Randy was scared of her.

As time went on, Vida's body began to weaken. Breeds like hers are especially vulnerable to fallen tracheas. Her windpipe got so narrow that air had a hard time passing through. Our whole family including Vida, of course, was out in Los Angeles the day she got into trouble. I was just finishing up a short vacation and was scheduled to fly to New York the next day for work. I was spending my last afternoon in the Jacuzzi with Jack, who was five, and Benny, who was two, when Vida showed up and, in full flying-squirrel mode, leapt into the bubbling water with us. I quickly took her out. I expected her to shake herself off or roll in the grass the way she always did when she got wet. But a few minutes later, Ben, who was Tom's assistant at the time and our good friend, came running with Vida in his arms—she was shivering and could barely breathe. I was frantic. I couldn't leave the kids alone, so I asked Ben to please rush and take her to the vet, saying she needed to go to the emergency room *right away*.

Taking Vida and Jack to visit Daddy at training camp, 2008.

When they got to Dr. Lisa's, she immediately sedated Vida. The vet told Ben that Vida was having a harder and harder time breathing because her fallen trachea at this point meant that her windpipe was no bigger than a straw. Vida needed to stay sedated at the vet's for observation, and my heart broke that I had to leave the next morning for New York—where I had a contract to fulfill. I was hoping that this was just a bad dream and that Vida would bounce back, but when the vet called me the next day to tell me Vida was getting worse and might not make it, I excused myself—*I'm sorry, I'm so sorry, I have to go*—and took the next flight back to LA.

When I got there, Vida was still heavily sedated—it was the only way she could breathe—and she wasn't moving much. She and I spent the whole day together. In the back lawn of our house there's a small waterfall area with a fishpond, surrounded by trees. It's secluded and peaceful. I wrapped Vida up in a blanket and she and I sat there until it got dark. I cradled her while she went in and out of her sleep. The last thing I wanted was for her to suffocate or be in any pain. The vet had told me she'd come to my home that evening. When she arrived, Vida was still in my arms, wrapped up tight in her blanket.

I placed a small heart-shaped rose quartz crystal inside the folds, along with my favorite scarf, which Vida loved to sleep on. I put my mouth very close to her face and said, *Thank you, Vida, for taking such incredible care of me. Now it's my turn to take care of you. You are going to sleep now, and when you wake up, you won't be in your body anymore. Thank you, little Vida—thank you, thank you, thank you.* Dr. Lisa couldn't have been gentler, kinder, or more respectful. My best friend took her last breath in my arms. I couldn't stop crying. I buried her along with a few of my favorite crystals, wrapped around the scarf we both loved.

Before I met Vida, dogs had always been a big part of my life. Growing up in Brazil, I had a few mongrel dogs—Xuxa, Suzy, Fofo, Preto—and after moving to LA in my early twenties, I went to the South Central pound, where I rescued Hazel, and I also had Willy and Django. When I first introduced Vida to Tom, Tom told me *he* wanted a dog, too. A big male dog! My guess is that some of his teammates were making fun of him for bringing Vida to practice. Through Petfinder we found Lua and her brother. I told Tom I was sorry, but I was *not* getting two new dogs. I was pregnant, and we already *had* two dogs in Costa Rica. Tom's sister Nancy offered to take in Lua's brother. Then, a few years later, Tom mentioned that since he was a kid he'd always wanted a beagle. Within days a beagle materialized in our front hallway as if by magic. Scooby was three years old and Tom said he was a rescue. He knew if he said the word "rescue," I couldn't possibly make a fuss, and I didn't. That's also how I found Pepe and Negrita, two dogs I brought in off the street in Costa Rica, who now live down there full-time. (If I find a dog or a cat or any animal abandoned on the street, there's no way I will leave them there to suffer, which is why I had so many dogs and fourteen cats as a child.)

A few weeks later, my friend Sam who lives in LA called to tell me that a friend of hers had found a few puppies abandoned in the street, and knowing that the other three puppies had homes, I did take one. Vivi named the new puppy Fluffy, but everyone calls her Fluffers.

I've loved every one of my dogs. I love my dogs today. But I've never loved a dog as much as I still love Vida. Today in our house outside Boston I keep a small altar where the heart-shaped rose quartz crystal that I tucked inside Vida's blanket at the end of her life still sits. I didn't want to bury it with her. I want to keep a part of her with me always. But I needed to bury her with the scarf we both loved. I told myself it would protect her from the cold earth and keep her cozy and warm. That rose quartz crystal is the one physical reminder I have of our last day together. Vida gave me thousands of joyful

Saying goodbye to my best friend, the day she left this earth, LA, 2012.

memories I will never forget. It may sound crazy to say that one small dog could be a guardian angel, a best friend, a protector, a defender, and a constant source of joy and happiness in my life—but it's true. Vida was the most loving, sweetest, smartest, funniest, most courageous little being I've ever known. Not a day went by when she didn't make me feel special, and happy, and loved. I know Vida can hear me when I tell her, over and over again, *thank you*. Mommy will always love you.

4

Our Thoughts and Words Are Powerful—
Use Them Wisely

One intention I try to carry out every day is to live my life with the greatest possible awareness—of myself and everything happening around me. This means being fully present while experiencing the moments of my life *as* they're happening. I think self-awareness is one of the most important things in life. But of course it isn't a goal so much as it is an ongoing process. When we're in our teens, many of us believe we know all there is to know about ourselves (and maybe everything else as well—just ask your parents). But a few years later, when we think back on that adolescent self, it can feel as if we're observing a stranger. Who *was* that girl anyway? I actually find this experience happens every few years or so. Our self-awareness has the potential to deepen and expand, and the biggest influences in this process are our thoughts, words, and actions.

What were the first thoughts that went through your mind when you woke up this morning? Did you feel grateful to be alive? Did you appreciate the warmth of your bed and how good it felt to stretch your muscles after a night's sleep? Did you look forward to the day ahead? Did you focus on all the work you have to do, and how you never have free time for yourself, and how the world sometimes feels like it's conspiring against you, and is it *really* raining again? I bring up these examples to point out that positive or negative thoughts shape the quality of our experiences.

Our thoughts create our words and our actions. In fact, using words is a kind of action. My understanding of the power of my own thoughts deepened tremendously when I began meditating. The more aware I became of where my thoughts were taking me, the more aware I became of the words and actions that followed. I realized that I sometimes felt at their mercy. Aren't our minds supposed to serve *us*— not the other way around?

Exhausted! Getting ready for a show in the early a.m. during hectic show season, Milan Fashion Week, 1998.

If your thoughts are positive, your words will tend to be positive, too. If your thoughts are negative, your words have a higher probability of doing harm, even if that was never your intention. Once we say something, we can't take it back. Saying things that are negative and damaging can hurt beyond that particular moment. Your words can become a part of *their* belief system, part of how *they* define themselves and you. What could be more dangerous than that? I tell my own children that their words are no different from spells. If love and kindness are be-hind those words, they become charged with positivity and can have a magical effect. But if their thoughts and words arise from anger or jealousy, they can do a lot of damage.

Each one of us is like a hard drive that gets imprinted with data. That data comes from our previous experiences. Was your home lov-ing and peaceful? Were you raised with a good role model of how people should treat one another? Or did your family members raise their voices and slam doors whenever a problem came up? It can be hard to shake free from childhood conditioning. By now you know I have close relationships with my own family members, but my rela-tionships at school were a different story. It was in school that I first learned about the power of thoughts and words.

When I was twelve or thirteen, I was a foot taller than anyone else in my class, male or female, and that included my own twin sister. My classmates continually teased me, making me feel weird and un-comfortable in my own body. I weighed around one hundred pounds. I used to wear two pairs of pants to school to make my legs look thicker. To distract from how tall I was, I went around with hunched shoulders, which of course only made my height more noticeable.

The last thing I wanted was to be different. I just wanted to feel like I belonged. School is the first time most of us are introduced to the idea of *categories*. Am I an athlete, an artist, a math whiz, a scientist, a theater person, a cool girl? I wasn't part of the cool group, but I was lucky to be a good volleyball player, which helped me a lot with my confidence and made me feel like I belonged to at least one group.

Still, some of my classmates really liked picking on me. They had different nicknames for me. The favorite was "Olly," after Olive Oyl, the tall, skinny character from the cartoon series *Popeye*. Another was "Saracura," which is a local Brazilian bird with tiny eyes and sticklike legs. I was also called "Camarão," which means "shrimp," since my skin turned bright red whenever I played an intense game of volleyball. I remember once walking into my classroom and seeing a poster that featured a drawing of a skeleton and underneath it someone had written, "Has anybody seen Olly?" I felt humiliated. Of course, the way I looked affected my social life, too. At friends' parties, I was rarely asked by boys to slow-dance and would stand there feeling left out.

Since I didn't know any better, there were times that I took my classmates' words as the truth. I would come home after school and

My last year playing volleyball with my teammates, 1994. That's me up at the net, spiking the ball.

gaze at my own reflection in the mirror. *Maybe I am a little strange*, I'd think. I didn't have the emotional maturity back then to understand why anyone would want to deliberately hurt another person. After all, my own father told all of us that if we didn't have something good to say about someone, we shouldn't say anything at all!

Only later did I understand that the bullies at my school only made fun of the kids who didn't blend in with the crowd. The girl with the red hair. The boy with the freckles. And in my case, the tall, awkward, skinny girl. They must have been unhappy with themselves, or with their own lives, or maybe they just liked to tease vulnerable kids to make everyone laugh. Or maybe they were projecting their own hurt and suffering onto me as a way to feel less alone with their own pain. I find it hard to believe that anyone who is happy or loving would ever bully someone else for the sheer joy of inflicting misery on them.

Obviously I haven't forgotten my classmates' words. But I've forgiven them, and haven't held onto any resentment or bad feelings. If I'd let those words define me, I would have stopped believing I was good for anything. When I got to São Paulo, I thought that was the end of it, since being tall and skinny now seemed to be a good thing. But then I heard the words of a fashion editor during one of my first castings: *She'll never be on the cover of my magazine. Her eyes are too small and her nose is way too big for her face.* I was so sad, and that day I called my dad to tell him what had happened. He said, "The next time someone tells you that, you tell them, 'I have a big personality, too.'" Somehow, hearing my dad's words made me feel much better and gave me renewed confidence. I always remember those words whenever anyone says something mean to me. Yes, I do have a big personality, and that I see as one of my strengths.

Still, at fourteen I was very much a tomboy—thin, muscular, and healthy, with normal-sized breasts—but then I hit puberty. Two years later my breasts got a lot larger, which made me stand out again and feel even more self-conscious, especially during a time in fashion when pale, androgynous-looking models were getting all the jobs. I was close to five feet ten, somewhere between 115 and 118 pounds, and very skinny, with massive boobs (they even nicknamed me "Boobs from Brazil"). At fittings, none of the sample sizes were made for women who were built like me. As a result, I wasn't feeling pretty or worthy—never good enough. But the negative words that people used to describe me were also motivating. From that point on, whenever I was offered a job I told myself I had to be more than good. I felt I needed to rise to the occasion every time and earn people's trust. Yet I still felt weird, and awkward, and could barely believe it when anyone in the business gave me an opportunity and hired me for a job.

Becoming a mother has stirred up vivid memories of my childhood. Benny and Vivi are still very young, but I have told them that the words other people use to describe them are only true if they accept them as true. For example, they might want to respond by saying, *Uh, no, actually, you're wrong, this is the truth about me*, instead of letting someone else define them.

The process of learning to define oneself isn't always easy, especially when you're young and your identity revolves a lot around what other people think and say about you. Still, I emphasize with Benny and Vivi that the choice of self-esteem is theirs and that most of the time, the words people use to describe us are projections of what *they* are feeling about themselves. After all, maybe when negative words

Fantasy versus reality, *her* versus the real me. In front of a Versace Jeans campaign, shot by Steven Meisel, 1999.

are directed at us, the other person is just having a bad day, and is simply venting his or her frustration.

Benny is one of those kids who gets upset if someone steps on an ant. If a kid falls down on the playground, Benny is the first one to rush over to make sure they're all right. Every morning when he arrives at school, Benny gives his friends a hug. But he's gotten his share of teasing, too. Imagine being the son of a famous New England Patriots quarterback *and* going to school in New England *and* being someone who'd rather draw, sing, and build with LEGOs than play sports. My own experience growing up has been good preparation for me to help Benny navigate school, and a situation for me to learn compassion for my younger self. Everyone is unique, and in time we start to learn about our natural gifts, what delights and motivates us, as well as what aspects of our personality we need to work on. I explained to Benny that Daddy is very good at throwing a ball, but he only became great at it after years of practice and dedication. Mommy is a warrior for the environment, Jack is a great soccer player, Vivi is a leader with her friends, and you, Benny, are a very good artist and singer. Benny seemed happy to hear that, but I know there will be many more conversations about this topic.

In fact, one morning last year when I was making the kids breakfast, out of nowhere Benny, who was at the table, said, "Mom—what's a celebrity?" It took me a moment—where had he even *heard* that word?—but finally I told him, "A celebrity is someone who works at a job that's more visible that other jobs. Doctors, dentists, teachers, farmers—they all do very important work." Daddy, I reminded him, has a very visible job playing for a professional football team whose Sunday games are often televised. "It doesn't mean the person doing that job is more important," I went on. "It just means that what they do is more *visible*." Benny seemed to accept this—*oh, okay, Mom*—but it made me think about what he might be hearing at school about Tom and me that he doesn't tell us about. Later I told Tom how important it is to talk to Benny about what Mommy and Daddy do for a living. It was time. So we did. Tom told Benny how hard he works and reminded him that he was one of the last people picked in the NFL draft back in 2000. *It wasn't like I was always good at this,* Tom said. *I studied. I practiced and then I got better and better at it. Benny, know that as an eight-year-old kid, the more you dedicate yourself to something, the better you become at it.* In response to the question Benny didn't ask, but must have wondered—How do people even know my dad's name?—Tom told him that people know his name, and like him, because they like what he does, or because they love sports. But that doesn't mean they really *know* him, not the way our family knows him.

Think back to the words other people have said to you. Those words had the power to hurt you, inspire you, motivate you, frighten you, comfort you, cheer you, make you doubt yourself—or make you feel understood, appreciated, and loved. Like most people, I've used words both positively and negatively. I've said things in anger and spoken words with love. Most of the time I try to set a steady emotional tone, but still I've said things I wish I could take back. I am far from perfect, but the good news is I keep on practicing and I do learn from my mistakes. Again, what are we all here on earth for, if not to learn? It's important to remember that whenever you treat yourself unkindly or critically, you are only hurting yourself. Change doesn't come from being judgmental or from putting yourself down. It comes from inspiration, from the desire to want to do better, to try again, to give it your best. When you learned how to walk, did you immediately run or jump onto an escalator? No, you took a single step. Maybe you stumbled and fell. You got up again. Next time you took two steps. Then three. *That's* how we all learned how to walk. That's also how we learn about ourselves and how to navigate life.

No doubt my most negative words have been reserved for family members, especially my sisters. Unfortunately, family members know one another's tender spots, and all too often can cause emotional hurt. I remember a fight with Pati on Skype, although I forget the exact details—it had something to do with me thinking Pati was being overly controlling or disrespectful. I got really angry, in fact I was barely aware of what I was saying—the words flew out of my mouth before I could stop them. I began with, *Well, then, let me tell you what I think about you!*

My intention was to hurt Pati, and I did. After all, hadn't she hurt me first? In the silence that followed, my twin sister was speechless. I was, too. I felt regret right away. That was such a cheap shot. The call ended. We both hung up feeling terrible. I couldn't get to sleep that night. I kept thinking what an idiot I was. I love all my sisters. Why had I been so mean? My justification—*But Pati was mean to me first! She started it!*—suddenly seemed lame. There were so many other, better ways I could have dealt with the situation, like saying, *I'm sorry you feel that way about me,* or *Why don't we speak again tomorrow?* I didn't need to slam my sister, but I had, and I spent the next day or two incredibly upset.

How do we apologize to someone we love, whose feelings we've hurt badly? A few days later when Pati and I spoke, the first words out of my mouth were *I'm sorry.* Pati thanked me and accepted my apology, but for the next week or so there was a definite strain between us. I knew it was my fault. I hadn't been self-aware enough to set the right tone, and I hadn't acted in a loving or respectful way, which is how I like other people to treat *me.*

There have been situations since then when I've gotten angry, but I've mostly learned to pause and reflect before speaking. Tom and I don't argue much, but sometimes, when I feel anger rising in me—growing, growing—I become aware of what's going on. Instead of reacting in a way I'll regret later, I remember to breathe. Then I'll tell Tom it's better if we talk later and I leave the room. Meditation has been key in helping me with my own reactivity. I think of my anger as a visitor, and I can see that it is potentially destructive, so I make the conscious choice not to engage with it. The next time Tom and I are together, we can revisit whatever we were talking about in a loving, respectful way, and we always do.

Sometimes instead of verbally reacting, I'll write a letter. My dad taught us that whenever we felt confused or unclear about something, we should seek out a quiet space and put our thoughts and feelings on paper. *When you are done,* he said, *read it and you will see things more clearly.* Once, when Tom and I were having a rough time, I got an email from him that hurt my feelings. He was in Boston at the time, and I was in Costa Rica. Instead of retaliating by sending a hurtful email back, I took out a pen and a piece of paper, and for the next hour I wrote down my thoughts and emotions, the things that made me angry, the things that made me frustrated—everything I was feeling at that time. I didn't censor myself. It was nonstop, no restrictions. When I finished, I was shocked to see I'd written almost three pages. I also felt relief.

It's much more helpful to me when I write my thoughts out in longhand. It's between me, my pen, and my paper. Writing by hand also eliminates the danger of impulsively pressing Send and then not being able to take my email back. The words in front of me felt honest and intense—crazy-intense, actually. Just writing them down made me feel a hundred times better. In the end, I never sent the letter. I let a day go by. Then I read what I'd written a few more times. That night, I rolled up the letter and burned it. It was as if by writing the letter, my turmoil had left me and gone into my writing hand, onto the sheet of paper—and then the fire burned it all away. The next morning I sent Tom a brief email telling him I was only willing to be in a relationship that was based on love and respect, and that I looked forward to us talking whenever he was ready to speak to me in a loving and respectful way. A day later, we did just that.

O ne of the greatest benefits of self-awareness is the access it gives us to our own inner voice. We all have one, even if at times we ignore it or remain totally unaware of its existence. Our inner voice is very private and unique to us. Its purpose, I've always believed, is to protect us, help us stay true to our values, and urge us to do the right thing. I believe each of us has a higher, more evolved self within. Often, if we listen to our inner voice, we come to realize that our higher self already has the answers to our questions.

When I was young, my grandmother told my sisters and me that we each had our own star in the sky. *How do I tell which star is mine?* I asked her. *It's the one that shines the brightest to you,* said my grandmother. No matter what you call your inner voice, or what form it takes—your star, your guardian angel, your creator, your God, your highest self—it is always looking out for you.

Your inner voice is always there to remind you that you are not alone. Its goal isn't to ensure we play it safe or never have fun. Sometimes, in fact, it pushes us to take risks. These days, before I make any decision, I check in with my inner voice. It needs to signal to me a quiet *Yes, this is the right thing to do,* before I move forward.

Trying to find space in the bed, 2008. That's Vida in back, Willie up front, and Hazel relaxing next to Tom. (Of course, this is *before* we had children.)

As our self-awareness gets stronger, our inner voice does too. Today I'm still relatively young and lack the self-awareness I hope I'll develop in the future. Still, I do realize this much: the better we know ourselves, the easier it is to find out what we're good at, what motivates us, and what brings us the greatest joy. As everyone knows, life can have a *lot* of chapters. A doctor can decide to become a philosopher. A firefighter can choose to become an actor, or the other way around. And a girl who grew up believing she'd play professional volleyball, or help sick dogs and cats, can become a runway model. Some things *do* stay the same, though. I still love animals, and on the rare times you find me behind a volleyball net, I'm as intense a player as ever. (If my shoulder didn't dislocate every time I played, I would do it more often, but I'm fixing that problem, so pretty soon I'll be back having fun and playing all the sports I love.)

Once you recognize and appreciate the things you're good at, it becomes much easier to focus on what exactly it is that you want to make happen and, even more important, why. That process begins with paying attention to your inner voice—though first you need to make sure that voice is really *yours*. Not the voice that tells you you're *supposed* to do something or act in a certain way. Not the voices of your mother or father. Not the voices of your teachers. Not the voices that trickle down from society, from your peer group, or from any organized belief system. Not even your inner critic, the one telling

My maternal grandfather and grandmother in front of their house—my favorite place to spend holidays when I was a kid—with my sisters and me, 1982.

you all your faults. No, *your* inner voice is the one that more than any other gives you a kind of *knowing*.

I admit that sometimes it seems confusing, because a lot of voices can be talking at the same time. One voice might be saying one thing while another says something else. How do you know which voice to follow? My advice is first to become as quiet and still as possible. Then pay attention to what your body is telling you. When you think about what the first voice is saying, do the muscles in your shoulders stiffen? Does your stomach feel funny? Now consider what the second voice is saying. Does your body feel more relaxed and open? Does your breathing get steadier? Listen to your body. Ask yourself, *Will the voice I follow keep me up at night—or will I be able to go to sleep feeling good about myself?* I follow the inner voice that fills me with peace, lets me sleep well, and makes me feel good about myself the next morning. If the decisions I make are based on love, and the actions I take reflect that love, then I'm being true to my inner voice. But there have been plenty of times when I've ignored that voice and paid the consequences, small and large.

For example, I've had wavy hair since I was a child. But when I started modeling, straight hair was the trend in fashion. So a friend took me to get a flat iron that made my hair straight, and I used it every day. I just wanted to fit in and look cool, like all the other girls around me. At sixteen, when I moved to New York, I was suddenly surrounded by a lot of girls who weren't straightening their hair, and I finally felt it was okay to stop. It was a liberating feeling to let my hair be just what it was. It's so funny that today something I'm known for is my natural hair texture.

Another time was when I was fourteen and decided to move to São Paulo. I thought I knew myself pretty well. I was a good girl. I had my head screwed on straight. I knew the difference between right and wrong. I wasn't going to fall off the rails. I also felt protected somehow. Someone or something was always looking out for me—I was convinced of it. Before I left home, my parents made it clear that they trusted me. They knew I was responsible and dedicated. I was a strong student, the captain of my volleyball team, and a good helper around the house. They also knew I would never do anything to disappoint them. Plus, a month earlier my dad had even written a long letter to Elite, my first modeling agency, to tell them he was entrusting them with his daughter.

I packed a single suitcase and backpack with everything I owned, and my dad put me on the bus, though not before giving me fifty Brazilian *reais* for taxi fare once I arrived in São Paulo. Twenty-seven hours later, the bus pulled into one of São Paulo's four massive

My first guitar. I always wanted to play just so I could sing along, as one of my favorite memories from my childhood was when my dad would play for us. Home in New York, 1998.

terminals. When I got inside the station, my first response was, *Whoa.* There were more people in that one bus station than there were in all of Horizontina. It was overwhelming.

I wandered around the terminal for a while, dragging my suitcase, just staring at the people and the signs. My dad had given me strict instructions. When I got to São Paulo, I was to use the *reais* he'd given me to take a taxi to the models' apartment. *Immediately.* My inner voice couldn't have been clearer or more in agreement that this was the right thing to do. In fact it was the *only* thing to do. *Find a taxi. Go to the models' apartment.* Just then I was aware of another voice: *Gise, if you're planning on going to castings, you need to wear the right clothes.* I didn't own even a single pair of jeans that fit me right. All I had in my suitcase was my school uniform and a few T-shirts and pairs of pants I'd inherited from my older sisters. How could I go to castings looking like that? Clothes had never mattered to me, but now, surrounded by well-dressed city people who looked like they knew what they were doing and where they were going, I felt the need to spruce up my appearance. Why did I have to follow my inner voice?

As I stood in the middle of the station, I came up with a new plan. If I took the subway to the models' apartment, I could use the money that was left over to buy a few pieces of clothing that actually fit me, and that would actually be *mine.*

In those days—1995—there were no such thing as cell phones. I couldn't call my dad and go over my new plan with him, and even if I could, I probably wouldn't have. I felt independent, and in charge of my own life. I followed the signs for the subway, bought a ticket, and stood on a crowded train car with my suitcase next to me and my backpack hugging my shoulders.

São Paulo is an enormous place. It's so big that it can take three hours or more to get from one part of the city to another. I asked people for directions, changed lines three or four times, and, by the time I got to the subway station closest to the models' apartment, I felt both incredibly intelligent and incredibly proud of myself. I'd outwitted the voice in my head and found *my* voice. But when I took the backpack off my shoulders to get my wallet, it was gone.

I'd left my backpack shut, but the top now flapped open. My wallet with the money in it hadn't dropped out; someone had stolen it. As if I was in a dream, I left the subway station and went outside. The streets were hot and smelly. I crouched down on my suitcase and burst into tears. It wasn't just the missing money that upset me, though that was bad enough; it was that now I had no ID either. Thank God I still had the slip of paper with the address and phone number of the models' apartment. But I didn't have any money to make a call at the pay phone. A woman passing by saw me crying, and when I told her what had happened, she gave me enough change to call my parents. My dad answered the phone. *Hi, Dad*, I said. *It's Gise*, and I started crying again.

My dad was furious with me, and who could blame him? I'm sure he must have been incredibly worried, too. I had ignored my inner voice—not to mention my dad's outer voice—and as a result I'd made a stupid decision. It was a devastating thing to do to my parents. They had trusted me, and I'd let them down. Even if they'd wanted to help, they were twenty-seven hours away. Fortunately I had enough change left over to call the chaperone at the models' apartment. I was by the subway, I told her. Would she mind giving me walking directions?

It took me nearly an hour to get to the apartment. São Paulo in

January is sweltering hot, and I dragged my suitcase for ten very long blocks, red-faced and sweating and feeling like a failure, though luckily most of the route on Teodoro Sampaio was downhill. No one seemed to notice I was crying, and I remember how strange that felt, since in Horizontina people would have stopped and asked me what was wrong and if they could help. I finally reached the models' apartment, met the chaperone, found my bed, and settled in.

From that point on, things got better. Three other girls were living there, and though at sixteen and seventeen they were slightly older, we all got along. I slept in a bunk bed. The first few nights were scary, since it was the first time I'd slept in a bedroom without my sisters. The modeling agency paid my rent and gave me an advance for my living expenses. The other girls liked me in part because I was always cleaning the apartment. (Even back then I couldn't help myself.)

I went to a fashion retail store and bought a new pair of jeans and a white T-shirt, which I wore every day and washed on weekends, and it became my new uniform for all my castings. I bought a map, and began figuring out the times and locations of my castings. I spent hours analyzing what subway or bus I needed to take to get here or there. Pretty soon I'd memorized almost every bus and subway line in the city. Within a month, I knew São Paulo cold. Whenever new girls showed up in the models' apartment, I was able to take them under my wing and tell them the best ways to get around.

I had ignored my inner voice—the voice that was telling me the right thing to do—and when I didn't listen, I made the wrong decision. I sometimes experience my own inner voice as a feeling. If I'm able to breathe quietly and calmly, then I know it's serving me well. If my breathing is shallow or ragged, it's a good indication something is wrong. When I decided to use the fifty *reais* my dad had given me

What can I say, I just love cleaning! In the models' apartment in Tokyo, 1995.

to buy myself some new clothes, I thought I was being smart, but I knew it didn't feel right. Not in my head, not in my body. The wisdom of this inner *knowing* feeling became even clearer ten years later, in 2005, when I was making the decision about whether I should continue working for Victoria's Secret.

I was nineteen when the company offered me a five-year modeling contract. When that offer came in, *Vogue* had just named me Model of the Year. I remember showing up for the ceremony in my hippie shirt, broken Birkenstocks, and usual oversize, ripped, comfy jeans. When Anna Wintour saw me, and asked if I had something to wear, I said, *Yes, this*, so right away she asked Grace Coddington, *Vogue*'s creative director, to find me a better outfit, though I'll never forget those expressions of shock about what I was wearing. In those days I was a fashion model, and Victoria's Secret was a catalog company. In 1999, there was a strong division between the two. Either you modeled clothes for Alexander McQueen, Versace, Dolce & Gabbana, and other high-end brands, or you worked commercially. There was no crossover. But when Victoria's Secret told me the terms of the contract, I was so happy! Working with Victoria's Secret would give me financial security for the first time in my life and a steady job for five years. I wouldn't have to do one hundred shows a year anymore. No more flying to a new city every few days. No more worrying about job offers drying up or about my own financial future.

For the first few years, I felt comfortable modeling in lingerie, but as time went on, I felt less and less at ease being photographed walking the runway wearing just a bikini or a thong. Give me a tail, a cape, wings—please, anything to cover me up a little! As time passed, I felt more and more uncomfortable. But I loved the people I worked with there, especially my dear friend-turned-Cupid, Ed, who had hired me and who many years later set up Tom and me on a blind date.

By 2006, thanks to a contract extension, Victoria's Secret and I had been together for seven years. My work with them still made up 80 percent of my annual income. The company told me they wanted to extend my contract for another two years.

To everyone around me, it was a very easy *yes*. Victoria's Secret

Taking pics to show my family back home while working for three months in Tokyo, 1995.

and I had had a long, trusting, mutually beneficial relationship. But I couldn't decide whether to stay or go. When you work for a company the size of Victoria's Secret, modeling is only part of your job description. There's also a lot of promotion. Store openings and in-store appearances. Television and print commercials. Coast-to-coast travel. Backstage interviews. Photo shoots for the catalog as well as for the website. Whenever Victoria's Secret introduced a new lingerie line, fragrance, or catalog with a special theme, it was my job to help promote it. If the company flew me to a remote beach in Virgin Gorda to model the latest swimwear line, a tabloid TV show would also be on hand to chronicle every step I took. I was certainly grateful for the opportunity and the financial security the company had given me, but I was at a different place in my life, and I wasn't sure I wanted to continue working there. A few months later I still hadn't made a final decision, and now it was time to make up my mind.

Every time I thought about my decision, my stomach got tight. If I renewed my contract, that meant I would keep on having to live my life on the company's terms. There wasn't anything I could do about their vision—Victoria's Secret was a huge corporation, and the train there ran at full speed—and they couldn't change my vision either, and the way I felt. That night before bed I prayed, *God, please show me the way. Give me a clear sign. Should I leave? Should I stay? What should I do?* Was leaving the right thing to do? Should I hold firm to my own beliefs? Was I sabotaging my own career? The next morning, I was no closer to a decision than I'd been the night before. I meditated for thirty minutes, asking myself the same questions over and over. Every time I did, my stomach felt tight.

Looking back, I think I was hoping that someone else would make my decision for me. That someone else, of course, was my inner voice—or my star, or my guardian angel, or God. Today I tell Benny and Vivi, *When you pray, look for your star. Pray every night to your guardian angel. Maybe tomorrow you have a test in school—well, then, ask your guardian angel to protect you. If the angels are messengers of God, talk to them, or go straight to the top and talk to God!* I remind Benny and Vivi that they can pray to the sky outside, or inside a church, or in their beds—anywhere, anytime.

I felt guided and it came to me in a flash. I crumpled up two small pieces of paper and placed them inside an empty teacup. On one paper I'd written the word *yes*—which meant I was staying. On the other I'd written the word *no*—which meant I was leaving. I closed my eyes and set an intention: whatever piece of paper I chose would be for my highest and best self and be the right decision. I reached in and picked up the one that read *no.* This was a confirmation.

No was the answer I unconsciously wanted to hear. It was also the answer my *body* wanted to hear and, I believe, had been trying to tell me for days. From that point on, I was at peace. I believed, trusted, and accepted that I'd made the right decision—or at least the best one for me. The tightness in my stomach vanished and didn't return. That same morning I got on the phone with my agent and the team at Victoria's Secret, and I thanked everyone repeatedly. I was incredibly grateful for all they had done for me during the past seven years. It had been a great opportunity and an amazing ride. But I wasn't going to renew my contract.

Sometimes there's no clear explanation *why* something feels right—but I believe you still need to follow what your inner voice is telling you. In the end, I was able to use the time and energy I'd spent working and traveling and devote it instead to what would become two of the greatest blessings in my life: my marriage and my children.

The more we trust our intuition, the stronger it gets. When I first began meditating, I discovered that I could put aside all my stress and anxiety and find a level of peace I hadn't known before. I still use meditation to get to that place, but I also use it to guide me and show

Saturday morning the right way! Three little angels in New York City, 2017. That's Jack in the back, Benny in the middle, and Vivi up front.

me the way forward whenever I'm confused and need clarity. I find that if I'm patient and give the process enough time and space, the next step always becomes clear.

Which is why when anyone asks me for advice, the first thing I say is, *Get quiet, find your inner voice, and listen to it as carefully as possible.* Avoid taking things personally. People will say things to you—and about you—but try not to let their words affect you. Other people's words have almost nothing to do with you and almost everything to do with them. Instead, ask yourself: *What do I really want? And* why? Be as clear as you can about your intentions.

Find your inner voice, listen to it, and keep refining the practice. The more you listen to it, the stronger it becomes. Stay true to your inner voice. It will remind you that you are never alone. And I promise it won't ever steer you wrong.

My friend and yoga teacher Cris practicing chanting and meditation in Costa Rica, 2008.

5

Where Your Attention Goes
Is What Grows

At the end of every year, on New Year's Eve, I make two lists that together sum up what I've done over the past twelve months. The first one spells out all the things that made me proud—learning a new skill, polishing up an old talent, being a good and present parent, mastering a sport or an activity that once scared me, launching a social or an environmental project, or taking the positive results of one I started earlier to the next step. The second list is devoted to areas that still need improvement. That night, I like sitting in stillness for an hour. I meditate on those two lists. Where in my life have I done well? In what areas do I think I came up short, and why? Are the places where I gave my fullest attention—my marriage, my children, my work, my nutritional and exercise regimen, my spiritual practice—in balance, or am I overdoing one while letting another slide? I also use my New Year's Eve meditation to set intentions and goals for the next year. Do I want to give up sugar (again)

Practicing yoga in Costa Rica, 2008.

for a month? Is there something I haven't done that I've always wanted to do? What scares me (which to my mind means I need to try it)? How can I become a better person, a better friend, a better mother, better at *everything* I do?

If it sounds like I'm tracking myself or keeping score, well, I guess I am. My New Year's Eve list-making is a form of self-analysis and a good way for me to measure my own development. I can feel good about whatever small victories I've achieved while reminding myself of the areas where I can still do better. It isn't a time for self-criticism. If I make that mistake, I reframe it as an opportunity for learning something new. It's also not a time to shower myself with praise. The big questions I always ask myself are: *How well or how poorly did I use the time I was given this past year? Have I taken full advantage of the hours, days, weeks, and months that I was given? Have I prioritized what is most important to me, and have I given my best, and most present attention?*

The lesson: *Where your attention goes is what grows* has always shown itself to be true for me. This is a very important lesson especially in a time when we're saturated with more information than ever before. It can take a superhuman effort to slice through the physical clutter and mental fog around us, in order to focus our attention on the things, and goals, that benefit us most and help us to grow. But the effort is worth it.

What we need to understand is that where we place our attention is within our control. From experience I know how easy it can be to allow other people to define us or limit our potential. If I had totally believed the bullies in my school or the people in the fashion industry who criticized my appearance, my self-doubt would have paralyzed me. Instead I focused my attention even harder on what I wanted to accomplish. Should we really allow other people to tell us who we are, where we're going, and what we're capable of accomplishing? Those people had no idea that the qualities that they were making fun of were the very ones that made it possible for me to be in this field where I have been successful for twenty-three years!

We all need to be careful with where our attention goes—and our attention always begins with our thoughts. Once we believe something is true, it becomes closer to coming true. If we have a poor opinion of ourselves, every encounter we have will be shaded by that belief. If we come into situations with confidence, our positive self-esteem will impact everyone around us.

As a girl, I realized I had no control over my growing body. What was I going to do, exactly—saw my legs in half to make myself shorter? But I could turn something I didn't like into something I did

Baby me.

like. Becoming a great volleyball player made being tall an asset. Plus I could become a good student and focus on where I could have a positive influence. But this mind-set meant that I had to overcome my own fears and insecurities—and this was especially true in my early days of modeling. The industry could be cruel in its treatment of girls. To some designers, models were hardly even human. We were hangers. I remember getting a job at age fifteen as a fitting model, where I had to try out the potential looks for a show. I had to stand naked, except for my underwear, covering myself the best I could with my arms folded over my breasts while someone went to get me the outfits. Sometimes they would take forever, leaving me there shivering. No one thought to bring me a robe or thought about whether I might feel self-conscious or vulnerable or cold. Since I was new to modeling and didn't know any better, I told myself that this was just how things were.

My first big break came in London. It was 1998. I was eighteen years old. Since the mid-1990s the trend in fashion had been known as "heroin chic"—lots of skinny, waifish, mostly androgynous-looking girls. I had nothing in common with that look—I was healthy and tanned and athletic, and I had big boobs. I was living in a models' apartment in central London where most of the other girls either smoked, drank, took drugs, or had piercings and tattoos. After three weeks and forty-three castings, most of the people booking the shows barely looked at me. They weren't interested in any of the modeling work I'd done in Brazil, not even a photo shoot where the hair and makeup artists had done their best to make me look boyish and cool. The heroin-chic fad was probably a response to all the healthy, athletic models who dominated modeling in the early '90s. I didn't know that the pendulum was about to swing the other way and that I was in a good situation to take advantage of it.

One day the agency sent me to a casting for the British designer Alexander McQueen's upcoming summer show. Lee, as his friends called him, had been chief designer at Givenchy before starting his own label, and even then he was considered one of the most creative, innovative designers of his time, known for a dramatic and unusual approach to fashion. When I got there, I joined hundreds, maybe even thousands, of other girls in a line stretching out the door and around the block. One by one, we made our way into a long hallway that led to a room where Lee sat on a couch. He had me put on a pair of super-high heels and a tight fishtail skirt and then had me walk for him. When I was done, he said, "Thank you," and nothing else. I wasn't sure how it had gone—and a few days later, when my agency called with the news I'd made the cut, I couldn't believe it.

The night of the show, I remember being struck by the fact that no one had called me in for a fitting. Maybe they'd figured out my dimensions from the fishtail skirt I had worn at the casting? I had done a few smaller shows in New York, but this was my first big international show, and I had no idea how it worked. That night I arrived at the venue feeling like I had crazy butterflies in my stomach. I sat in a chair as the hairstylist pulled back all my hair and fitted me with a black wig, and the makeup artist glued long black feathers on my eyelashes. I was pretty sure that at some point someone was going to come and ask me to try on the clothes. At that time—I was barely eighteen—my English was still limited. I could say "good morning" and "good afternoon" and "hi, how are you?" and "I'm fine!" and make out a few things people were saying to me, but most of the time I just nodded and smiled a lot, since the last thing I wanted was to look dumb.

Before showtime, it was chaos backstage, with a lot of stress and yelling. Soon it was time for all the girls, including me, to change into our outfits. We were given less than a minute to dress. I had three looks that night, three outfits—a stringy silver thing like a bathing suit but with chains hanging off it, a dress, and the fishtail skirt. None of them had been fitted on me. I went out wearing the first two without any problems, though it was definitely fewer clothes than I'd ever worn on any runway. Now it was time for the fishtail skirt.

Backstage, during a runway show, it's always rush, rush, rush. The rush to change clothes. The rush to touch up hair and makeup. The rush to line up and get back out on the runway. Someone pushed the fishtail skirt at me and I changed into it. My legs could barely maneuver in the skirt, and the height of the heels made it nearly impossible to walk. I was still waiting for my top, and in my broken English I finally asked someone where it was. "There *is* no top," came the answer.

I began to cry. I had no idea what to do. Mostly, I thought about how disappointed and embarrassed my parents would be. I tried to hold back my tears, but they just kept coming down, and the black feathers glued to my lashes began coming unstuck. I could hear the heavy crunching industrial beat coming from the runway. I thought about leaving, about running away. There was no way in the world I was going out there without a top. But if I left, I knew I'd probably never be given another opportunity. I'd be called unprofessional— that is, if casting agents bothered to call me anything at all. But in the end, it was my body, nobody else's.

As soon as Val, the makeup artist, saw the situation, she said she would *paint* a top on me using white makeup—which she proceeded to do. It *did* look like a top, too. Val told me how beautiful it looked and said that the runway was so dark no one would know I wasn't wearing a sheer white shirt. If Val hadn't shown up just then, I seriously doubt I could have walked the runway. I remember thinking that if anyone took photos of me, at least my parents wouldn't be able to recognize me in my black wig.

At one point I noticed that one girl, then another, no, wait, *all* the girls, were coming backstage with their hair soaking wet. It took me a few seconds to grasp what was going on. I could already barely move in my tight fishtail skirt and high heels. Now I was about to go out there in a painted-on top and it was also *raining*?

That was probably the night I started to dissociate, to begin thinking of my public self as *her* and *she*.

The Alexander McQueen show, 1998.

Because the girl who finally appeared on the runway wasn't anyone familiar to me. A few minutes earlier I'd been crying so hard my tears were washing off my makeup. I was a good girl. I was a tomboy. I was someone whose big breasts had embarrassed her since she'd hit puberty. I was a girl gripped by the fear that my family would feel so embarrassed they would never talk to me again. I was terrified. (Thank God that the internet wasn't that popular in Horizontina back then—my parents would have ordered me to come back home.)

I trained my eyes to focus on a single light at the end of the runway—and went out. No one saw the shy, scared, embarrassed, insecure eighteen-year-old girl that night. Instead, they saw a strong, confident woman in a skirt tight around her knees. *She* was managing to walk in impossible heels on an incredibly slippery stage. *She* didn't make any mistakes. *She* didn't fall. *She* gave off the impression she didn't have a care in the world. The rain made her black eye makeup run down her face, so no one could tell what was rain and what was tears. *Fake it till you make it*—I swear, it really *does* work! Thank God the whole thing began and ended quickly.

It turned out that walking in Alexander McQueen's show was the beginning of my international career. He was seen as a genius, the best, most innovative designer of his time. The industry considered him a visionary. He was revered by every fashion editor and photographer in the industry, and many of them were in the audience that night. When he picked me to be in his show, my agency told me what a big deal it was, though I hadn't really taken it in. During the actual show, I was on the runway, half-naked and crying as rain came down from the ceiling. Looking back, I must have really stood out, especially in contrast to the heroin-chic look everyone was used to. My boobs were big, and even though I was crying, I was healthy and fit. The industry was *ready* for a change. It was the right time, and that night I was the right model. I was different and the industry was *ready* for that difference.

In one night, I'd somehow managed to claim a spot on the fashion world map. All of a sudden, lots of people wanted to work with me. People started calling me the girl of the moment. It was somewhat overwhelming, though some people still felt free to criticize me to my face. After modeling in a few shows in Milan and Paris, I flew back to New York, where a handful of people appeared in my life who would be instrumental in my career. The first three were top fashion photographers, and one is still a legendary magazine editor. First, Mario Testino booked me to be on French *Vogue*. Almost that same week, Patrick Demarchelier booked me to be in *Harper's Bazaar*. Then I began working with Steven Meisel, who is not only an extremely talented photographer but an incredible teacher, who really taught me how to model. A year later *Vogue* editor-in-chief Anna Wintour put me on the cover of her magazine with the feature story "The Return of the Curve." *Vogue* is considered "the fashion industry's bible." When Anna made a pronouncement about a new fashion movement—in this case that curves were back—and chose me to illustrate that movement, it was an explosive moment in my career. I was one of the youngest models ever to appear on the cover of American *Vogue*. Inside was an Irving Penn photo of me nude.

At the time, there were three legendary fashion photographers— Richard Avedon, Helmut Newton, and Irving Penn, who rarely took pictures anymore and who everyone wanted to work with. When my agent told me that Irving Penn wanted to photograph me nude, I was extremely hesitant—I didn't want to take off my clothes. I also didn't know how to say no to the biggest, most influential fashion magazine in the world, and an icon, who was one of the three most important fashion photographers in the industry. The whole idea made me uncomfortable, but my agency said it was very important, and I said I would do it. Frankly, I didn't feel I had much of a choice.

Irving Penn, who was close to eighty years old when we met, was a genuine artist and a kind, respectful man. Normally during photo shoots there are more than a dozen people milling around, but he worked with only an assistant and Phyllis, the editor, and he shot using only natural light—at least he did the two times I worked with him. He was very courtly and old-fashioned. There was no retouching. Taking off my clothes wasn't easy for me. People might think that Brazilians fling their clothes off left and right, but I also grew up in a very Catholic family, and I felt uncomfortable standing there with nothing on. But I did what my agent said. I remember standing there naked, not moving, barely breathing, for almost two hours, with my face angled to the right. This also made me feel uncomfortable, since I'd convinced myself I only looked good from the left. "I don't think this side is so good, Mr. Penn," I said. I won't ever forget his response. In his slow, calm voice, he told me that everyone and everything has its own unique beauty—that *every* side is beautiful. When I finally saw the photo he took, I saw that he was right. The photo was different but also, at least to my mind, beautiful—though I literally couldn't move my neck for weeks afterwards. Years later I chose this picture to be the cover of a book I edited celebrating my twenty years in the industry. Working with Irving Penn freed me up in so many ways, not least of which was the realization that I looked different from other models—and that was okay.

Another way many people thought I was confident—but which was actually something else entirely—was my way of walking the runway. As time went on, I became known for what some people called my "horse walk." I would raise my knee high and kick my foot forward, which created the overall impression of a stomping mare. The truth is, I had no other choice. My feet are size 8, and I am five feet eleven. The high heels that models wear are towering, making it almost impossible, in my case, to keep my legs straight. Imagine being my height and balancing on small feet inside very high heels, and you'll understand that my horse walk was just a way for me to keep from toppling over. It had another effect, too: it made the girl modeling on the runway—*she, her*—feel proud, strong, confident, and determined. I looked as if I were kicking things out of the way. Never mind that the heels I usually wore were so painful to walk in that I took them off the moment I was backstage.

If before the Alexander McQueen show my attention was focused, afterward it became a laser. I'd known what I wanted, but now the possibilities seemed much bigger. I was committed to climbing the mountain I saw in front of me. As far as I was concerned, nothing was going to stop me. So what if one day I felt sick, another day I had cramps, and a week later I was going through a bad patch in my personal life? Even when I felt like crying, I showed up with a smile, ready to work. Modeling uses up a lot of people—I'd already seen so many girls come and go—and I wasn't going to be one of them. As time passed, it seemed healthier, and more protective of who I really was, to think of modeling not as my identity but as a business. Which, in fact, it is. To me, that meant I had to master every element of that industry. Hair. Makeup. Cameras. Lighting. Angles. The entire creative and collaborative process.

The best way we learn how to do anything is by *doing it*. Day after day, my job gave me the opportunity to be surrounded by teams of amazingly creative people. I had great teachers. I set out to absorb and analyze anything and everything I could. I would sit there paying close attention when someone was doing my hair or makeup. I watched the photographers closely and learned about lighting and angles, and found out quickly that when you change the lens and the angle, you change *everything*.

The *most* important factor for a photo to come out the way you want it to is lighting. In contrast, the angle is what makes a photo interesting or not. Is it a conventional front-facing photo? Is the photo shot from a lower angle, which has the effect of making me look taller, or shot from the top, which makes me look smaller? Or is the photo shot from one side, in a more deliberately artistic way? If lighting creates a mood, the angle can determine whether the photo is different, or unusual, or just plain commercial (although lighting can do that, too). So I began analyzing photos that were poorly lit: *that doesn't look good—why?* The more I understood about lighting and angles, the better my photos got. I could see how one beam of light complimented my face while another made it look weird, and how moving my chin a millimeter to the left or right subtly altered the entire effect. (I was always trying to find angles where my nose looked less pronounced and my eyes looked bigger.)

In the end, I gained a much greater understanding not just of my role in the collaboration, but also the parts everyone else played. Some people might have seen me as a hanger, but I was analyzing and trying to learn. Having worked with the top people in fashion for so many years also gave me the opportunity to help hairstylists and makeup artists with less experience. I knew what made me look good. *Maybe you could try putting the eye shadow this way?* I'd say. *Or my hair this way?* I wanted to help *all* of us. Luigi, a dear friend and probably the best hairstylist I've ever worked with, as well as being a great photographer, jokes that he loves being my hair assistant because I'm good at playing with my hair during shoots, as it helps me get into character!

By its nature, modeling is a time-limited, youth-oriented industry. Models face a lot of temptations and situations where they can easily slide off the rails. Most girls begin modeling around the same age I did, in their early teens, a time when they are heavily influenced by their peers. At that age, you just want to fit in, and in a business where there's a lot of partying, drinking, drug taking, and "glamour," where the emphasis is pretty much exclusively on how you look, that can be a dangerous combination. *How long are you going to be doing this, Gise?* I asked myself. Back then there was no good answer, but I knew one thing for sure: when the time arrived that I was no longer offered jobs, I wasn't planning on going home empty-handed. If nothing else, I wanted to own my own place. What was the point of paying rent when I could use that same money to get a mortgage and buy my own apartment? I began squirreling away whatever funds were left over at the end of each month. I'd never been interested in expensive clothes or handbags or shoes. I was more of a hippie. If I needed new clothes, I paid a visit to one of the downtown flea markets. Why buy new clothes when I was going to be dressing up at the studio? When I got more successful and clients began sending me first-class airline tickets, I traded them for seats in economy, and the money I saved went straight into my savings account.

That's how I was able to buy my first-ever apartment in New York, on Beach Street in Tribeca. It was a small apartment without much light, but I loved it because it was *mine*. After moving in, I didn't have much money left to pay for renovations, so I did most of them, following my mom's example of always trying to do everything herself. I sanded and stained the floors, and I did the same with four white benches I found at a street sale on Houston Street. Those four benches come with me wherever I go, and they sit today in our kitchen in Boston.

I furnished the other rooms at IKEA. To remind myself of Brazil, I bought standing trees and a fish. I *did* need to hire someone to renovate my bathroom, so for the next six months I took showers at the studio or at a friend's house. A lot of girls couldn't believe it when I

Fixing up my apartment in New York, 1999. After sanding the floors, it is time to stain them! I have always loved doing things like that. I have my own toolbox. And don't get me near a hammer; I love hanging pictures around the house.

told them I'd bought my own apartment. But I always kept my eyes straight ahead. I always knew what I was working for.

What we choose to focus our attention on is so very important. First comes the *thought*. Why? Because before you can aspire to something, or act on something, you need to imagine what that thing is. The more you think about something, the stronger your thoughts around it become—and eventually it turns into a *belief*. When I was having my panic attacks and drinking mocha Frappuccinos, smoking a pack of cigarettes a day, and drinking a bottle of wine at night, it became a kind of belief system. That belief system told me I was a person constantly on the go who needed to smoke all day to keep moving and drink wine every night to relax. That was what I believed I needed to do to keep going. Smoking and drinking wine were the actions I took *based* on that belief system. The cures—meditating, running every morning, and making changes in my diet—were actions based on my new belief system. I thought meditating and doing yoga could help me—and slowly, as they did, those thoughts evolved into a positive, life-altering belief.

Your thoughts can destroy you or your thoughts can catapult you to new and better places. But whatever you choose to do as a result of your thoughts, make sure you do it for the right reasons. When you do something to satisfy yourself, something you really feel will make you happier, it's a wonderful thing. But the moment you do something to just please other people, or society, or the culture, it can backfire on you, as I know very well.

As I said earlier, after the Alexander McQueen show, the fashion industry began referring to me as "The Body." I'd become extremely at ease in that body. But after my children were born—Benny in 2009 and Vivi in 2012—quite naturally my body began to change, especially after breast-feeding each child for almost two years. Although breast-feeding was one of the most special experiences of my life, and I am so grateful I was able to do it, on the other hand it not only made my breasts much smaller, it made them slightly lopsided. The fact is, no matter how healthy you are, or how regularly you work out, if you're a woman your body is going to change after pregnancy and birth.

Besides that, I wasn't nineteen anymore. I was in my early thirties, and a young mother. For years I was labeled "The Body," and the fashion industry had high expectations for the way I looked. But time passes for all of us, and we all change. When I showed up for jobs, some people would make comments, indirectly or more pointedly. "What happened to your boobs?" they would say, or "Your boobs have gotten so small!" Some even suggested I add padding—what the industry calls "chicken cutlets"—to my bra.

Well, if where our attention goes is what grows, I now became preoccupied by the size and condition of my breasts. Suddenly I was very self-conscious about the way they looked. At the same time I had always wanted to give my best, and I felt somehow I was no longer able to live up to the expectations that others had of me. Still, it wasn't within my power to revert to the body I had before I had children. Which led me to make one of the most upsetting decisions of my life.

I never considered getting plastic surgery—even when people made comments about my nose, or my eyes, or made me feel inadequate. But this time around, unfortunately, I chose to give attention to the comments I was hearing. I decided to get breast surgery. My thinking was this: *If I get my breasts enhanced, no one will make those comments anymore, and I will feel like myself again.* I chose to trust my surgeon, believing he knew what was best for me. But—trust me—I have learned that no one knows better than *you* what is best for *you*. When the surgery was over, I no longer recognized my body. I became uncomfortable with the size of my breasts. I felt angry and depressed. Why did I do this to myself? Why did I let my attention go there? I'd done something, for myself, but mostly to try to please others. The lesson here is to listen to yourself first, to be clear about what you want, before making important decisions. After all, you will be the one living with the results.

If, on the other hand, our attention focuses on positive things,

Getting painted by several beautiful Kisêdjê women inside their tent, Amazon, 2006.

it will grow in positive ways. For example, I've always loved nature, but it wasn't until I visited the indigenous tribes in the Amazon in Brazil in 2004 that I came face-to-face with the crises created by deforestation. My visit was profound, and eye-opening, and when I left I told myself I had to do something to help preserve the natural resources. I asked Grendene, the Brazilian company I worked with for years on a line of sandals, to please help me bring attention to environmental causes. We decided that a percentage of our annual profits would be donated to help protect the Xingu River, which flows into the Amazon, and to help support various other environmental causes, including the regeneration of forest, water, and endangered species in Brazil.

I wanted to do all I could to bring attention to environmental problems, so we also partnered with a group in America to create a web cartoon series for kids called *Gisele and the Green Team*, about a group of teenage girls who live double lives as supermodels and environmental superheroes. In Horizontina my dad and I created Agua Limpa, whose mission is to regenerate the water quality. This effort led to some awards and recognition. The United Nations asked me to be one of their Goodwill Ambassadors. Harvard University also took notice of the work I was doing. Years later this work led me to give a speech at Rock in Rio. In the past few years, much of my attention has been focused on working on behalf of the environment, as my concern for the earth and future generations is enormous, and I hope to inspire everyone to help.

I bring careful attention to the information I take in every day—and how I feed and nourish my own mind. As a public figure, I know there's a lot written about me online, almost all of it by people who don't know me. Some of it is negative and unkind. Online, people

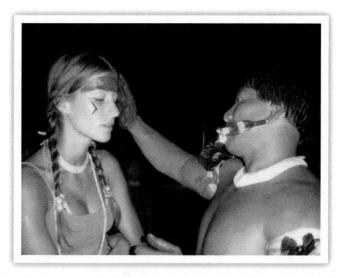

The first time I went to visit the Xingu region of Brazil in 2004, the tribal chief of the Yawalapiti people stained my forehead with *urucun*—an indigenous plant—in preparation for the night's ceremony.

make comments about other people they don't know, comments that they would never express if they were face-to-face. Computers are machines, and emails, texts, and online remarks detach us from the idea that another human being is on the other end. Anonymity doesn't just create detachment; it also seems to facilitate cruelty. It's hard for me to believe that anyone with a happy life would go online for the sole purpose of saying nasty things about someone they don't know. This is worse than the kids who bullied me in middle school, because the number of people who make comments online is much larger. Happy people have better things to do.

My whole life I've thought of myself as a happy person. I'm fortunate; I have my husband and children to love, and work I still need to accomplish. If I gave all my attention to the internet or the latest breaking news, the quality of my life would change, and not for the

Me, speaking—and, as usual, getting emotional!—talking about the *Água Limpa* project in Porto Alegre, Brazil, 2008.

better. My phone would become my focus, and my fear, anxiety, and helplessness would grow. In my twenties I remember having awesome days at work or with friends, and then getting home and turning on the TV or going online and seeing something that upset me so much I became really down for the next few days. Focusing too much of your attention on the news, or on the internet, or on anything outside yourself, can consume you. It isn't your life, but it might as *well* be your life. If you keep giving your full attention to things that make you fearful or anxious, you will become more fearful and anxious.

On the rare occasion that I check the online news, I often find myself reading words or watching images that remind me of the stray floating thoughts I'm aware of during meditation. They come and go from one hour to the next, one day to the next. It can be helpful to ask, does letting your attention focus on this or that information benefit you, or connect you to your best, highest self?

W hen I was asked to take part in the opening ceremonies of the 2014 FIFA World Cup, I was torn. Like a lot of Brazilians, I believed Brazil could have used the money being spent on stadiums and running tracks for other, more urgently needed things, like improving hospitals, schools, and the infrastructure. But in the end I said yes. I felt it would be an honor to represent my country, as an opportunity to make a positive contribution. I thought, not for the first time, that darkness is nothing more than the absence of light. All my attention was now focused on trying to give off as much light, hope, and positive energy as possible—and to represent my country in the best way that I could. I had the same feeling when I was asked to walk the runway at the opening of the 2016 Rio Olympics. My goal— and I hope this doesn't sound too grandiose—was that I could serve somehow as an inspiration, a positive image for Brazil. It would be a privilege, in fact, and I would experience something I would never have the opportunity to experience again. I *had* to do it.

When I got to Rio and took the car to my hotel, I couldn't help overhearing what they were saying on the radio. All of it was negative. No one believed Brazil could host a successful Olympics ceremony. As a result, I was apprehensive about the whole situation. But I also knew that whenever I'm afraid of stretching myself, that's when I need to be brave. If I'm unwilling to dare or try something new, I close off opportunities to experience the benefits that could come about as a result. The biggest successes in my life have all come about when I reached beyond my own comfort zone.

My task at the Olympics was to walk more than four hundred feet by myself. Just me. No one else. Thousands of people would be crowded inside a dark stadium, and millions more around the world would be watching on television. Many things can happen, or go wrong, in four hundred feet. What if I fell? Thank God I have never fallen during a show, but I knew it could happen. I'd lost a shoe, broken a heel, and gotten the tail of my dress caught in my heel plenty of times, but I'd never fallen. Before going on, I said a short prayer.

I asked for protection, strength, and courage. I asked to be a conduit—a messenger of light and love. Then the glare of the spotlight hit my head.

When I felt that light, I was aware of the enormous positive energy in the darkness around me. Behind a center-stage piano, Daniel Jobim, the grandson of Antonio Carlos Jobim (Tom Jobim), the great Brazilian composer who introduced bossa nova to the world, played and sang his grandfather's song "The Girl from Ipanema" as I began my walk. It may have just been me up there on the stage, but every one of my guardian angels was walking with me. The world might have been watching one woman walking a darkened runway, but I didn't do it alone, not for a second.

I like to embrace every opportunity that life gives me. I like to challenge myself, to experience new things, because we never know how much time we have left. Time is our biggest gift, and I don't want to waste any of it. We have only a limited number of hours, days, and years to experience the magic of this life, the beauty of our planet, and the sensation of being inside our bodies. My relationship with

Praying backstage, just before my runway walk at the Olympics opening ceremony, Rio de Janeiro, 2016.

time—and my feeling that there's never enough—lies behind my impatience and also my self-discipline. There is still so much I want to do!

Because time is precious, I often reflect about how to use it wisely. *How am I using my time? Am I spending it with the people I love? Am I being mindful and present in each moment? Am I learning about people, ideas, or situations that will feed me in a positive way? Am I reading books or magazines that teach and inspire me and bring me joy? Am I focusing my attention on things that might be out of my comfort zone—but help me grow?* The important point is that we can choose to put our attention on the areas of our life that will support us being our best.

6

Nature: Our Greatest Teacher

In Horizontina, where I grew up, there were no traffic lights. No movie theaters. The roads were mostly cobblestone, with the exception of the main one, where there was the hospital, also the bank, where my mom worked, and SLC, the heavy agricultural equipment factory that employed most of the residents and was later taken over by the machinery company John Deere. The closest town wasn't much bigger, with only about thirty thousand people, and Porto Alegre, the state's capital city, was seven hours east by car.

Many of us look back on childhoods that seem simple and innocent and joyful—maybe because *we* were!—but my childhood actually was. In my town everyone knew everyone. Cars would slow down when the drivers saw us jumping rope in the streets, and people would chat with one another. There was no such thing as a locked door. At age four I toddled over to the house belonging to our neighbors Karina and Melissa, let myself in, and fell asleep watching cartoons on their couch with my bottle by my side. It was that kind of place. But more than its friendliness and safety and the freedom my sisters and I felt walking home from school or riding our bikes wherever we wanted, I remember most being surrounded by nature. The fruit-bearing trees, so many different birds, the rows of blackberry bushes, the warm grass, the sand when my parents took us to the ocean on vacation, the mud under my bare feet, and above my head always the huge, warm, brilliant sky.

When I say, *Nature is our greatest teacher*, you might wonder what exactly nature teaches us. *Nature* is a pretty big category after all, and we grow up learning about it in pretty disconnected ways. In science we might memorize types of leaves or cloud shapes, or learn about our solar system or the moon's effect on the tides. Social studies teaches us geography and borders and population growth. Not many people link together what these subjects have in common: *nature*.

Maybe the better question to ask is, what *doesn't* nature teach us? To me, nature is *everything*. She is the highest, greatest expression of creation, love, and compassion. No matter how many times I watch the sunrise, or hear the rain falling, or see a wave rolling into shore, or a flock of geese flying, I'm completely awestruck. In order to stay alive, to eat, drink, breathe, and absorb light from the sun, we need to maintain a continuous exchange with nature. If the flow of this exchange is interrupted, *we* pay the price. Nature gives us life; without her, none of us would be here. When did we start forgetting that our lives depend on this exchange?

Like most people, I grew up believing church was just a place you went on Sundays. But why confine God to a man-made structure? I believe nature *herself* is our church. She is certainly mine. If you attune yourself to the energies of love, compassion, and service that nature provides, you can see God—who is, I prefer to think, the creator—in everyone and everything. It's as if by giving us life, the lakes and oceans, the trees, fields, and deserts, creation wanted to experience *itself.* Nature is intelligent. She is in balance. She is patient. She is wise. I believe that if we got into the habit of devoting even a few minutes every day to restore the connection between ourselves

The power of trees. In the Amazon rain forest, 2011.

and nature, we would feel a profound and positive shift. I know that in my own life this connection brings me incredible peace and joy.

I believe that we can choose to live in heaven or hell right here on earth. Both are in our own minds. We are helping create either one. Rather than letting other people decide whether you're good or bad, the choice is up to you. If we can all agree God is love, then everything that is unloving is the opposite of God.

We are living in an information age. I don't think it is a coincidence that it seems like today more than ever people are disconnected from nature, and from themselves. We forget to go outside. Instead of going for a walk, sitting on a rock, listening to a stream, or strolling on the beach, we are using an app or a video that duplicates those experiences and sounds. Most of us have trouble just *being*—being with ourselves, being with other people. When was the last time you went out for lunch or dinner and no one took out their phone? There's a quote I love that says we have only two ways to live our lives. One is as if nothing is a miracle. The other is as if everything is a miracle. Nature shows me that *everything* is a miracle.

My whole life I've been susceptible to what I call "energy." The energy other people give off. The energy I pick up when I enter a room. Everyone and everything releases some kind of vibration. I know I'm not alone in this experience. A lot of people are sensitive, some more than others. No doubt science has an explanation for it— or maybe a way to dismiss the whole subject—but nothing felt more real to me than the energy I was aware of, starting when I was very young.

As a little girl trying to get to sleep at night, I sometimes felt a presence in the bedroom I shared with my sisters. A sensation of heat or cold. I couldn't see what I was feeling—I didn't *want* to see it—but

I could sense it. Those presences were like the sudden hot and cold pockets of water your skin touches against when you're swimming in the ocean or a lake. Anytime I felt one in my bedroom, I dove underneath my blanket, or whispered fiercely to Pati or Gabi to wake up, wake up! or else I'd jump onto the bunk underneath mine, where Fafi slept. Whatever it was scared me. I didn't want to think about what it could be. But those presences were as real to me as going to school or playing volleyball or doing my chores.

With Benny in our garden, 2013.

Humans are seekers of knowledge. We are searching for ways to understand ourselves and make sense of the world—ways that might be different from what we were taught. Maybe what we're looking for are experiences that give us meaning and a feeling of connection. Nature makes me feel that way.

Nothing gave me more joy when I was young than helping my grandmother in her garden, or climbing a tree, or when I was immersed in the ocean water when our whole family went to the beach. Nature was as tangible a presence as any one of my sisters. Whatever energy I was giving off seemed to vibrate in harmony with her. Nature wasn't ever something *other* than me. She *was* me. She is *all* of us.

This feeling from childhood has never gone away. Every moment I spend in nature reminds me of how my little place in the world connects to something vast and awesome. All I need to do is take a walk behind my house, or see a bird flying in the distance, or go surfing in the early morning, and nature brings me back to balance. She nurtures my soul.

Most of us don't really *see* trees. We treat them as scenery, part of our landscape. We seldom stop to think about what trees actually represent. Aside from being beautiful, they take in carbon dioxide, storing carbon and releasing the oxygen that we breathe. They trap pollutants in their branches and leaves. In the form of forests, they help create rain that balances our climate. They help shield us from ultraviolet rays. They offer shade, which cools roads and houses and lawns. They give us the wood we use to build houses. They increase the amount of moisture in our air and slow down soil erosion. They give us food in the form of nuts and fruits, and they can contain powerful medicines and poisons within their leaves or bark. The first home for many of us is a crib made of wood, and the last one a coffin, and in between many of us live in wooden-framed houses. Trees have provided the paper for this book. Just think about the miracle that is a tree. They are truly wonderful.

Now think about your own body. So many aspects of our body need to be working simultaneously for any of us to be alive! Our hearts beat; our lungs take in and expel air; our veins circulate blood, oxygen, and nutrients; our immune and lymphatic systems fight off infections; our digestive system breaks down food; and our brains orchestrate the entire process by sending messages out to every part of our bodies. Do we ever stop to think about how miraculous that is—and how miraculous *nature* is? I tell my children that God, or our creator, is the energy of love that comes from abundance. The

Benny and Vivi planting trees, 2015.

evidence of that love, and creation, is everywhere, and in everything. It's in the day and the night, the rocks and the grasses, the trees and the plains, the planets and the oceans. It's in you, and me, and all of us. God created nature—and nature is God.

When I think back to the panic attacks I had in 2003, I wonder if they would have been as bad if I hadn't been spending all my time in a city. Manhattan buildings close off the sun and sky, whole blocks are in shadow, and artificial lights and pollution blind people from seeing the stars at night. During my panic attacks, all I wanted was to be in nature. I found myself longing for the little cabin I used to have in Woodstock, New York. At that time, on free weekends, or sometimes just for the day, I would drive up there by myself, with Joni Mitchell playing on the CD player. Once I was there, I'd spent most of my time outside, walking, soaking in the sun, gazing at the nearby pond, listening to birds, and now and again catching a glimpse of a black bear, aware all the time that nature was healing me. I'll never forget how the earth seemed slowly to pull away all the tensions that had built up during the week.

Nature—and my reverence for it—is still a large part of my day-to-day life, and that includes my mealtimes. Before I eat, I always bring my hands together over my plate, close my eyes, and say a short blessing. As I said, I believe everything is alive and gives out energy, including my food. If I'm eating a salad for lunch, I focus on the fact that everything in front of me—the lettuce, the carrots, the beets— were once seeds. As those seeds grew, they were warmed and nourished by the earth, the sunlight, and the rain. Now they're nourishing *my* body. The least I can do is have gratitude and honor that cycle.

I say thank you to my food and ask that it nourish every part of my being. I end my blessing by saying thank you three times. (Why three times? I don't know. It just became a habit.) Only then do I start eating.

Vivi doesn't think much of my ritual, but Benny says a blessing now, too, and Vivi will sometimes. None of us is automatically entitled to food, and I don't ever want to take for granted what's on my plate. Too often we gulp down what's there without thinking, as we're reading or watching television or playing with our phones. Blessing my food before I eat means that I'm giving it my fullest respect and attention.

When I'm in Costa Rica, my favorite time to go surfing is at five a.m., when no one is around except the pelicans and dolphins. I always ask permission to the ocean before going in. What am I to the ocean? A little speck. That's why before I enter the water I take a few moments to say a short prayer. I ask the ocean's permission to swim in it and for its protection. I feel I'm creating a contract between us, as well as showing a respect and reverence for the water.

To be perfectly honest, every time I go surfing, I'm afraid. Afraid of sharks. Afraid of being pulled under by a strong current. Afraid of drowning. As a kid, I used to go in the ocean a lot and loved jumping into the waves. One day I was swimming in the ocean with Gabi and Pati and our cousin Lisi, who was the oldest. I didn't know it was dangerous to swim near the rocks, especially because the currents were strong, but I was young, and the tide was high. Gabi was swimming next to me, and then a moment later I heard her scream. Without even thinking, I paddled toward Gabi, and then both of us were caught in a powerful current. Pati screamed for help, and Lisi tried to grab us, but then she got trapped. About twenty people were standing on the beach. They somehow managed to form a human rope and pulled us onto shore. I'd never felt so helpless, or afraid, in my life, and for years after that I stayed out of the water. But as I got older, I really missed being in the ocean, and wanted to go back to having fun in it. At first, I went in only as far as my ankles, before taking a seat in the sand. One day I decided to buy a surfboard, so I could at least float on something. I've now been surfing for many years. So far, the ocean has taken extremely good care of me, and I've certainly experienced joy from being in its presence.

Visiting my grandmother's small farm as a girl played a big part in developing my love and reverence for nature. My grandmother planted and grew most of what she ate, and season by season I watched as the seeds she'd buried in the soil and nurtured became sprouts and, later, vegetables or individual herbs, which she traded with her neighbors. I grew to appreciate how one season produced one fruit or vegetable, and the next season another crop entirely. I could see the cycles of nature at work, the long journey a seed traveled to become the food on my plate. Spending time on her farm was when I first realized that everything on our earth is alive, whether it's a blade of grass, a grain of rice, or a piece of fruit, and that I should appreciate everything and never take anything for granted.

From my grandmother I also absorbed the importance of eating locally grown foods. One of the biggest disconnections from nature that I see is the way most people shop for groceries. It's common to buy fruits, vegetables, meat, seafood, and poultry without knowing where they came from, or whether the producers have added chemicals and stabilizers to the food. Most of the produce my family eats comes from local farmers and growers. I'm a big believer in eating locally grown food and, to my way of thinking, no two jobs are as important and underappreciated as farming and teaching. If you think about it, farmers and teachers are similar. Farmers grow and nourish the food we eat, and teachers grow and nourish our children's minds!

Local fruits and vegetables taste better, because they are fresher, since nothing has to be added to them to keep them from spoiling.

Eating locally is also better for our environment. It means that the food we eat had to travel a shorter distance to reach our tables. I know it's hard for some people to find local produce—especially people who live in urban settings—but I'm always happy to read that farmers' markets are on the increase. Once you taste the difference in local produce and can feel your own energy level rise, it's hard to go back to eating any other way.

Breakfast snuggles in Costa Rica, 2015.

We're lucky to have our own small garden behind our house in Boston. Growing our own vegetables and herbs has been a wonderful experience for all of us, especially the kids. In the same way I began to understand the cycles of nature at my grandmother's farm, it's begun to dawn on Benny and Vivi that life doesn't just happen—that there's a process, and a rhythm, to everything on earth. For a cucumber or a strawberry to grow, it needs sunlight, rain, fertile soil, and, of course, lots of love and attention. Whenever Benny and Vivi have a friend from school over, one of the first things they do is run outside into the garden and pick and eat a baby cucumber or a cherry tomato right off the stem. Whenever they do, I'm reminded of my own childhood. It feels like a complete circle.

Is there a better teaching tool than a garden?

Having a garden has also taught my children about the challenges that face any living thing. We have a wonderful gardener who comes to help us, and Benny and Vivi like to help her place ladybugs on the plants, so they can ward off predators. They understand how plants are endangered by voles or rabbits or the occasional deer that jumps the fence. As the children get older, they take more and more pride in helping prepare their own food and meals. They understand that the vegetables and herbs we grow in our garden play an important part in nourishing *their* bodies. They also understand that some of their favorite fruits—blueberries, strawberries—just aren't available sometimes because they're out of season. They hear how hard it can be for local farmers in the fall or winter, and the challenges of growing produce in a greenhouse, and how, say, a sudden heavy snowstorm or ice storm can cause a greenhouse roof to collapse. As a result, they

Tom—with Vivi helping—checking out the new beds we added to our garden in the back lawn of our house in Boston, 2017.

are more understanding of the effort, commitment, and love that goes into being a local farmer.

In the future, I'd like to learn more about botanical medicine, since some of the most powerful medicines available to us come from nature. Having grown up with a mom who made special teas whenever my sisters and I got sick, I've always been fascinated by the ways nature can cure us. I'm not against Western medicine, but on the rare occasions that I don't feel well, I always choose a natural medicine. If I get a fever, it follows that my body is trying to tell me something. Sometimes just sitting in a tub in room-temperature water is a great way to bring my temperature back to normal. If I get a headache, I first drink a lot of water, and then I lightly massage some peppermint aromatherapy oil onto my temples. Even better is lying down for a short time, and usually my headache goes away.

My own grandmother was something of a medicine woman. My mom told me that when anyone in her small village would get sick, they would first call my grandmother to find out if they could be treated with herbs, rather than going to the hospital, which was far away. If any of us girls had the beginnings of a cold or flu, she would make teas and put peppermint oil under the soles of our feet, cover them with socks, and send us to bed. When we had a cough, she would cut up an onion and place the slices in our room or pin them to our pajamas. Along with making sure we stay hydrated and get massive amounts of vitamin C, I do this for Benny and Vivi when they come down with fevers. In my experience, it works. A few times, when the kids have had the beginnings of a sore throat, I've used a method I learned from my mom. I pour really cold milk onto a cloth, cover the outside of the cloth in plastic wrap, and arrange it around her throat. It's a little stinky the next morning, but Vivi's sore throats are usually gone—I have no idea why. Also, lemon is a natural disinfectant, so if anyone in my house is sick, I cut a lemon in two and leave it faceup on the dresser next to the bed. In the winter I also like making a tea out of manuka honey, three or four chopped-up lemons, and freshly grated ginger, especially if the kids or I feel the beginnings of a cold.

And if one of the greatest lessons that nature can teach us is about the rhythm of the seasons, well, imagine what it's like being a Brazilian woman surviving a New England winter! Ten of them so far! If I had to choose between winter and summer, I wouldn't have to think twice. Nothing makes me happier than being barefoot and wearing light clothing. Having grown up in a tropical climate, I would naturally prefer to live where it's warmer, but I also love the beauty of the seasons in New England. Still, the winter can be tough. I don't get depressed because of the darkness, but I'm freezing all the time, and I'm a person who literally turns blue when I get cold. But once I learned that the secret to surviving cold weather is layers—sweaters, down jackets, ski pants, jackets, socks, gloves, leaving only your eyes visible—winter can be a beautiful, cozy time of year. I like to ski, too, which I've been doing regularly for about four years, though when I was learning I spent most of my time on my butt. Benny and Vivi are already both better skiers than I am, and Jack flies down the mountain, which reminds me how good it is to start learning a sport (or, for that matter, a language) as early as possible. Me, I still stick to the blue runs!

I may spend the winter months dreaming of warmer weather, but Benny and Vivi, who were both born in Boston, love winter, especially going outside and making snowmen or snow angels or having snowball fights. They're hardy New Englanders. Sometimes even when I'm wearing three layers of clothing, I still feel cold, whereas

Vivi, who's wearing only a sweater, tells me she's boiling. My favorite times in December and January are when it's snowing outside but I'm indoors, wearing fuzzy sweatpants and cozy socks, sitting before the fire, reading a good book—but to be honest that rarely happens, since I'm usually running around doing a million different things. Nature is beautiful and inspiring, no matter what season.

She—nature—was also my inspiration when it was time for me to have my cubbies. (Even their middle names are inspired by her: Rein [rain] and Lake.)

I'd always dreamed of giving birth naturally, at home. To me it is the most peaceful, beautiful way for a child to come into this world. Ever since my twin sister, Pati, got double pneumonia when we were ten, I've had a strong aversion to hospitals. The idea of giving birth at home not only felt natural and right, it also connected me to a deeper sense of power. It was about trusting my own body, and my creator, to bring a new life to the earth. It wasn't as though I was the first person to consider this idea. Until the 1900s, millions of women gave birth at home. When I was pregnant with Benny, though, many people reminded me that very few women today give birth at home. Well, I guess I was going to be one of them.

A few years before I got pregnant I met Mayra, a very special young woman who was studying to be a midwife. Mayra told me that unborn babies basically float in water inside their mothers—and that the gentlest, most soothing way for a newborn to enter the world was into water. That stuck with me. I knew after that conversation that I wanted to birth my baby in water. I told Mayra that I would love to

In the kitchen of our former apartment on Beacon Street in Boston. It was 2009, just a few weeks before Benny's arrival.

have her with me when I had my baby. A few months before Benny was born, I called Mayra and said, "Are you ready? Let's do it!" Some women, Mayra told me, have given birth in the ocean, while others have given birth in a bathtub. I chose the bathtub option—an easy decision, since it was December, and the middle of winter, in Boston. I began watching lots of videos that she recommended of women giving birth in the water. At first, most people around me, including Tom, thought the idea was dangerous. But my mom completely supported the idea, and was with me when both my children were born.

Tom and I were in Los Angeles with Jack during the off-season when I had my four-month checkup with an obstetrician. The doctor told me that it was too dangerous for me to have a home birth. He said that Benny was in an unusual position, my hips were too small, and the odds just weren't in my favor. He said it was probably best for me to schedule a C-section. And as I said, Tom wasn't enthusiastic about a home birth either. Only after I had him watch a half-dozen natural-birth movies did he finally agree. (Or maybe Tom just didn't want to have to watch one more natural-birth video.)

I told the obstetrician that I was going to have my children at home. My attitude was the same as it had been in middle school: *I don't think you get to decide this!* No one was going to talk me out of it. I began doing more research, and soon I found Deborah, a very knowledgeable midwife. She had attended hundreds of at-home births. She was also kind and loving, exactly the sort of person I wanted by my side when I delivered my baby. Deborah explained to me where Benny was in my uterus—she wasn't worried—and reminded me that I had no health issues and that I was young and totally capable of doing this. She had no concerns and was confident that I would have a successful home birth.

My plan was to give birth in my bathtub, though I'd overlooked an important fact: I'm five eleven, and the bathtub was, well, not a whole lot bigger than that. I was in labor with Benny for sixteen hours, and the last three I spent in the tub, as Mayra, Deborah, Tom, and my mom continually replenished the hot water. Any woman who has given birth knows it is one of life's most overwhelming experiences. But the more intense the pain, the quieter I got. The whole process was unfolding between me, my God, and my child. Krishna Das was playing softly in the background, and I was surrounded by flickering candles. I closed my eyes and kept focusing on my breathing, knowing that with each contraction, I was getting closer and closer. As always I had a purpose: I was finally going to meet this little being who I'd been carrying around in my body for nine months. I would get to see his little face! My clear sense of purpose made my pain more bearable. My whole life I'd been praying to my guardian angels, but when I was giving birth, I went straight to God.

When Benny arrived, I felt, but not for the first time in my life, that I was somehow outside my own body experiencing the moment from two different perspectives. I could see myself in the bathtub, as if I were watching a movie, witnessing it from above, while simultaneously feeling a rush of energy as I kept breathing. I was watching my son be born from a distance, and yet at the same time I was totally in the experience of giving birth to him. I've always wondered exactly how that could be happening. Maybe it's because at that moment the veil between the earth world and the spirit world gets thinner. I don't know—all I know is that it was magical!

Me and my sweet baby boy, a week after his birth, December 2009.

Vivi's birth three years later was slightly different. Having learned my lesson about the bathtub, I bought a birthing tub, almost seven feet in diameter, which came with a water heater. It not only kept me warm, but it also gave me enough room to move around. Unless a woman is very small, I would recommend buying or renting a birthing tub (I gave mine to Mayra, so that other expectant mothers could use it). Once again, Krishna Das was chanting, and the candles were glowing. Tom was in the tub with me, and my mom, Deborah, Mayra, and my sister Fafi were also in the room. I'm so happy that I was awake, and conscious, when I gave birth to both my children. Yes, the pain was sometimes hard to bear, but focused breathing helped lessen the pain. Giving birth to my children at home were the two most extraordinary experiences of my life. I'd made a decision,

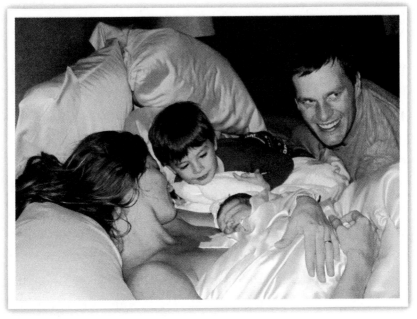

Right after Vivi's birth, Benny came to our bed excited to meet his little sister.

trusted myself that everything would work out, and it did. I am so grateful.

I remember lying in bed with each of my cubbies right after they were born and thinking, *Nature is miraculous, life is truly magical— and so are our bodies that can create life, and how incredible to feel an instant intimacy with a small being you have just met.*

I also noticed a new kind of strength within me. I felt like Kali, the Hindu goddess of time, creation, destruction, and power, a feeling of invincibility. I could chew rocks in half! I could split mountains in two! I could divide oceans! Kali is also linked with death. When a baby is born, a mother takes a step backward. A part of her dies. It was also the death of me-ness, of ego, of me putting myself and my own needs first. Birth is a metaphor for many aspects of life, because it takes much effort, and only after we have passed the test are we given a reward.

In 2008, I funded and worked with my dad on a program dedicated to restoring the quality of the water in a small river in Horizontina. We called it Projeto *Água Limpa*, or Clean Water Project. It was a very rewarding experience, not only because I got to work with my dad, but because it brings joy to my heart to know that we were able to create a meaningful, lasting change to that region where I was born. By regenerating the margins of the river, local people today have access to cleaner water. Recently my family decided to expand our efforts, using what we learned with Projeto *Água Limpa* to clean the Jacuí River, one of the largest rivers in our state. I'm thrilled to take on this new challenge, with the hope that in the future others will join this effort so that we can clean up more and more rivers in order to provide fresh, clean water for everyone. I hold the vision that we will be able to work together with local communities, which in turn will be empowered to care for and preserve natural resources.

Our health depends on the health of our planet. When we hurt nature, we hurt ourselves. No doubt nature notices our lack of awareness, and the countless ways we are abusing and destroying her, but she just keeps on giving. My wise friend Noel, who maintains the trees in Ireland's national parks, once gave me a simple and profound explanation for what is happening today with nature. "Any living thing that loses one-third of its skin," he said, "suffers a high fever and is at great risk of dying. To date, our earth has lost one-third of her skin—the trees, the soil, the ocean, and the biodiversity surrounding them. Yet instead of helping to grow and replenish what has been stripped away, we keep on pillaging and ravaging." Many people take the earth, the food we eat, and the water we drink for granted. Many more believe we're entitled to take everything nature has to give.

Vivi, my little girl, flying into the sunset, in Costa Rica, 2016.

We're not! We *all* need to contribute to the future of our planet. This is *our* earth. *Our* water. *Our* trees. *Our* future. If we're going to continue to live on this planet, it's *our* responsibility to roll up *our* sleeves and *do* something to help. It's up to *us* to protect the earth and save ourselves. *We* are the ones we have been waiting for. *We* need to honor the organism that supports us. *Our* future is in *our* hands.

So please, be as useful as you can. Use the special gifts that life has given you to serve others and make the world a better place. Remember, you and I and everyone who lives on this earth is a part of nature—and why are we here if not to learn, grow, and help one another?

7

Take Care of Your Body
So It Can Take Care of You

Before I start this chapter, I feel I have to address something, but I'll do it fast, because it makes me uncomfortable. I've been told that many women wish they had a body like mine. I also know that many people are curious about my diet. I must admit that I find all of this a bit strange. There are many things I really like about my body—I'm naturally athletic and proud of it—and many things I dislike, including my shoulders, which to date I've dislocated about *nine* times each. Many women have said to me that they wish they were as tall as I am. My height in the end turned out to be a big advantage (modeling! volleyball!), but it wasn't my choice to top out at five feet eleven. Especially when just trying to fit in as a teenager, it's hard to be unnoticed when you're a foot taller than most of your friends.

The body I have is the one I was given—remember four of my sisters are about a head shorter than I am—and all the kale and coconut milk in the world won't make them taller. A lot of people seem to be under the impression that I follow a special diet or a special exercise plan in order to look a certain way. The truth is when I was younger I didn't have to do very much to keep my body fit. I *am* a model after all, and my natural body type is leaner, with smaller bones. But at thirty-eight, my metabolism has slowed, and today, I am very thoughtful about what I eat. I have a healthy diet, and I exercise daily, for a simple reason: so I can feel good. Remember the anxiety attacks I wrote about earlier? They were an incredibly motivating force in my life. If you've ever had one, you'll understand that you never want to experience another. My panic attacks were much more motivating than any pleasure I might have from standing in front of the mirror.

Cooking my mom's special chicken vegetable soup, just a few days before Benny was born, Boston, 2009.

I know that there is a lot of confusion about what people should and shouldn't eat. The internet, in particular, is a mishmash of information, a lot of it contradictory and confusing. Remember when eggs were great for you, but then they were terrible, and now they are great again? Who knows what to believe? In the face of *Eat this, drink that—no, wait. Don't! Wait! Do!*, it's no wonder a lot of people throw up their hands. If all the experts seem to disagree about what's healthy and what isn't, we all just might as well eat pizza, hamburgers, ribs, bacon, chicken nuggets, ice cream, carbonated sodas, chocolate bars, and macaroni and cheese. Life is short, why not spend it eating whatever we want?

The thing is, we don't simply risk having a short life if we don't pay attention to what we put in our bodies, but we become vulnerable to illness and unhappiness.

My panic attacks completely transformed the way I ate. The first change I made was to cut sugar out of my diet for three months. That wasn't easy. My ninety-day no-sugar fast ended in July, right around my birthday. (I was born under the sign of Cancer, and we crabs like our food.) I remember showing up at a studio to discover that some nice person had brought me a small chocolate birthday cake (my favorite). I wasn't planning to reintroduce sugar into my life, but the gesture was so thoughtful that I didn't want to be rude. When I ate a small slice—the first sugar of any kind I'd eaten in three months—I felt sick and disoriented. I could hardly focus for the rest of the day. My doctor had reminded me that sugar was in bread, pasta, juice, crackers, cereal, granola bars, sodas, energy drinks—most processed foods contain a lot of added sugar. No wonder kids bounce off the walls when they eat a high-sugar diet. After my sugar cleanse one little slice of cake made me so hyper! The episode really showed me how bad this kind of sugar is for me.

Even after cutting out all types of sugar, caffeine, and alcohol from my diet, it wasn't until Benny was born that I began eating the way I do today. The knowledge that everything I ate or drank was passed to my baby through my breast milk, affecting his health, immune system, and energy, pushed me to refine my habits even more. I was no longer eating for just myself. For a while I got a little obsessed with the nutritional content of my food, though I have relaxed about it over time. (I will be the first person to admit that overthinking what you eat is almost as bad as not thinking about it at all.) Once I began making healthy changes to my diet, the rest of my family came along.

With Benny in Costa Rica, 2010.

Making nutritional changes happens at a different pace for everyone. I've noticed this with my family in Brazil—my mom, my dad, my sisters, and their families. Once a year we all come together for a family reunion, where the cousins can play and keep nourishing their relationships. We usually meet in Costa Rica. For years I provided healthy food options. At first, there were just a few complaints. Some family members used to go to the local supermarket to buy "extras," so they wouldn't be deprived of their favorite snacks and soft drinks. This used to upset me: *For only 10 days,*

Family reunion in Costa Rica.

can't we all just eat healthy food? Please? But slowly, as the years passed, and the family reunions continued, first some, then others, began changing their dietary habits, and today most of my family members are aware of what they eat, and how much better they feel when they eat healthy foods. Today I am so happy to see my sisters and their children eating good-quality foods. At this point, we are constantly exchanging healthy recipes on our What'sApp group. We also share natural remedies and health tips. These days when we all meet up, there are no more complaints about the food and everybody is actually excited about the menu!

When choosing what to eat, I think about energy and balance. By energy I mean maintaining my vitality, so that I can be my best both for the people around me, and for the work I want or need to do. This doesn't just mean performing well—but also feeling healthy and thinking clearly. This process requires self-awareness. Will a particular vegetable, piece of fruit, cut of meat, or dessert give me the energy I need and want, or will it make me feel tired and depleted? In my early twenties, when I barely ever thought about what I ate, I would usually eat a cheeseburger and French fries for lunch and a big bowl of pasta with cheese for dinner. Afterward, the only thing I felt like doing was curling up in a ball and falling asleep. To bring my vitality up after a meal, I'd drink a cup of coffee with lots of sugar, and when the caffeine wore off, I'd have a second one or maybe a third. After so much caffeine, I would start to fall apart both physically and emotionally.

Now I'm aware that I simply can't afford to feel tired or dopey, much less anxious or crazed. Time is in short supply, and I hate wasting any of it. If I eat poorly then I expend a lot of energy just trying to feel normal again. Why go there if I don't have to?

As far as balance is concerned, Tom and I both live by the old saying *Moderation in all things*. My husband likes to say, Too much of a good thing isn't a good thing—and too much of a bad thing is just plain bad. When you think about it, too much of anything, whether it's alcohol, caffeine, sugar, running, or sunlight—isn't good for any of us. This really is common sense. For example, once in awhile I might still drink one or two small cups of coffee, usually if I'm flying overnight and then going directly to a studio. The difference is that now I understand that caffeine is a powerful upper, and I treat it as such. On special occasions I might have a small piece of cake—but when I do I know exactly how my body will respond and I know there will be a price to pay. (Having said this, I do love sweets, but mostly I eat healthy desserts without processed sugar.) Now that

I have eaten a clean diet for many years, I experience the effect of sugar and caffeine as soon as I have any.

When I began thinking about food in terms of whether it gave or took away energy, I started to become more aware about what to eat or not eat. I don't call my nutritional regimen a diet, but rather healthy eating habits, so I can maintain a high level of vitality and the mental clarity to have a productive and enjoyable life. These same attitudes motivate my morning exercise. I don't work out only for the sake of losing or maintaining weight, but for a clear mind and an energized body. When I exercise daily I feel less stressed, plus my energy level increases, so I can accomplish all the things I want to do.

When I first met Tom, he mostly ate the food commonly served at his football team's cafeteria. Heavy-duty guy-food. But he was

Practicing yoga while pregnant with Vivi, 2012.

beginning to make a shift to healthier food, snacking on nuts and grapes. A few weeks after we met, Tom and I and his friend Kevin met for dinner at what was then my favorite place to eat in New York, a raw, organic vegan restaurant on Irving Place in the East Village. Most items on the menu were made out of dehydrated cashews. As usual, I ordered a large salad with different kinds of vegetables (and seaweed) with seed crackers on the side. "Do they have steak here?" I remember Kevin asking. When Tom was done eating, he wanted to know when his food was coming. It was kind of funny seeing these two big guys so confused about what they were eating, but the good news was that they both left the restaurant feeling satisfied, and it also became one of Tom's favorite restaurants in the city.

In 2008, Tom suffered an ACL injury in the first game of the season. He decided to have his surgery in LA in order to be close to Jack, who at the time was only a month old. It wasn't an easy recovery, thanks to a series of staph infections. Tom was in bed for months. I met a caterer on a photo shoot who delivered delicious, healthy organic food to the set. I asked him if he would be interested in working for us. He agreed and started delivering meals to our house three times a week. Once Tom started eating clean, delicious organic foods, he felt much better, and it wasn't too hard for him to give up his old diet. We both decided that we wanted to keep eating this way, even after we returned to Boston. We both felt stronger, more energized, and mentally sharp. I may have been the one to introduce Tom to a healthier diet, but since he's so dedicated and disciplined about being healthy, our preferences came together naturally.

Now our family's diet has evolved to be a whole-food, plant-based diet that ideally emphasizes organic and local ingredients, including raw or lightly steamed vegetables, fruits, legumes, and whole grains, with the occasional small piece of meat or seafood added into the mix.

The south of Brazil, where I grew up, is an area of the country with lots of plantations and ranches for breeding cattle. Growing up, I was a typical gaucha, a southern Brazilian girl who ate meat almost every day. Many years later—on two separate occasions—I tried to become a vegetarian. I love animals. It really bothered me that I ate them. The first time lasted nearly a year and a half. But I became extremely anemic, despite eating lots of beans, lentils, and chickpeas to make sure I got enough protein. My fingernails got flaky, and when I examined the skin beneath my eyes it was white instead of rosy pink. Even iron and B_{12} supplements didn't help and I felt tired all the time. When I told my doctor about my symptoms, he suggested

In the Amazon, during the filming of *Years of Living Dangerously*.

that I reintroduce meat into my diet. This was not what I wanted to hear.

Two or three years later I made my second attempt at becoming a vegetarian. I thought I could do it since my diet only contained a little meat. I lasted only ten months and then I got anemic again. Whether it has to do with my blood type or my body type or what, I'm still not quite sure, but I now accept that a vegetarian diet doesn't work for me.

Currently I eat meat twice a month, and seafood once a week. I pay careful attention to the source of my meat and the types of fish I eat. Ever since my doctor explained to me that larger fish, like tuna and swordfish, contain greater concentrations of mercury, we make a point of eating smaller fish.

I also love to cook. I used to cook all the time, in fact. Before I was married, my sister Fafi stayed with me in New York for four months. Every night when I got home from the studio, I made us dinner. (After all, I feel like I'm Fafi's second mom.) Today, my schedule is a lot busier and I need to prioritize, which means I don't often cook meals, but occasionally I do make time to prepare healthy desserts. We are incredibly lucky to have Susan, who comes to our house five days a week to prepare wholesome meals for the whole family. The kids love being with her in the kitchen, helping out and learning from her talent and tricks. With my mom living so far away, it's wonderful for Benny and Vivi to get to spend time with Susan. She's loving and nurturing, and her food is always healthy, nutritious, and delicious. Susan is also devoted to composting and eating seasonally and knows a lot about farming. She even helps the kids plant vegetables and herbs in our garden. Having learned that bees are dying because of pesticides, we decided to get two hives. We either use fresh honey or dates when we want to sweeten things. I've read that using local honey can also help relieve allergies! Most of our family's desserts are a blend of avocado and coconut. To my mind, those are the very best fats we can have. Whether we make ice cream or a mousse—and if I'm trying for my favorite extra-chocolaty taste—we use a combination of avocados, bananas, and 100 percent raw cacao powder, which creates a very creamy, delicious base.

As I wrote earlier, after oil-pulling and meditating, I begin my mornings by drinking a glass of lukewarm water combined with half a lemon. A half hour later, as I'm making breakfast and putting together Benny's and Vivi's school lunches—and if I haven't finished off *their* breakfasts—I'll drink a glass of green juice. Usually it's a blend of celery, cucumbers, half a red or green apple, turmeric, ginger, lemon juice, and occasionally kale or beets. If I'm having my period, I'll often just do beets and lemon for extra iron and vitamin C. If I plan on doing a heavy workout, I make myself a smoothie using either fresh or frozen berries, a spoonful of cacao powder, hemp seed, flaxseed, chia seed, and a splash of coconut milk. Sometimes I add a banana or a spoonful of homemade almond butter or protein powder. I also take vitamins and carry a small pack of them with me whenever I travel. In general I'd rather get my vitamins from the actual source, food. But I take vitamin C, a B multivitamin to protect against fatigue and possible anemia, and vitamin D to protect my bones. I also get acupuncture, and an intravenous shot of vitamins, including C, B_{12}, and magnesium, from my doctor in Boston twice a year. I usually do it before the winter starts, when we're all more prone to getting sick.

Twice a week, I make a point not to eat anything until lunchtime, even if I am working out. I always feel incredibly energized from this mini fast. It takes a lot of energy for our bodies to digest the food we eat, and I think it's a good idea to sometimes give our digestive system a rest. There has been a lot of information written about the benefits of fasting. I especially find that a liquid fast helps me when I get sick, when my body wants just soup or tea. I occasionally devote a month a year to going completely sugar-free, which includes fruit sugar and the sugars from any grains or alcohol.

I'm also a big believer in small portions, especially as I get older. A lot of people believe that in order to get strong and healthy, we need to eat lots of food. The opposite is true. Eating smaller portions won't overwhelm our digestion or exhaust us. When I was growing up, my mom told us never to leave the table until we'd finished all the food on our plates. She reminded us how fortunate we were to have food, and that many people in the world have none. For years I felt guilty whenever I left even the smallest piece of food on my plate. I would eat until there was nothing left, leaving me feeling stuffed and exhausted. Today, I just serve smaller portions that I know will satisfy me, without leaving me feeling overfed or tired. I also feel lighter, more vital, and ready to tackle the day.

Food is meant to energize us, not make us fall asleep. That's why my lunch typically consists of a salad, with seed crackers and avocado, or a bowl of soup containing chickpeas and many different vegetables. Another favorite lunch, especially in the summer, is homemade spring rolls with tahini sauce for dipping. Spring rolls are easy to make. I combine one or two slices of apple and avocado, chopped cabbage, and some shaved carrots and cucumber, and roll them up in a sheet of rice paper. Two or three rolls are usually enough to satisfy

Having homemade fruit popsicles with my girly girl, Costa Rica.

me. They are light, perfect, and delicious, especially with the sauce. I can literally drink tahini sauce, it's so good!

Despite what you might have read about how we eat, our family isn't 100 percent dairy-free. I happen to love eating goat cheese and sheep cheese, though I've stayed away from cow dairy ever since I had a test that showed I have an intolerance to it. I either drink coconut milk, which we make at home, or almond milk or hemp milk. Those are the three favorite milks in our family, with coconut being mine. When friends come over for dinner, I often serve a platter with cheese, nuts, and a little honey on the side. Not five pounds of cheese, mind you, but a small portion—a Midnight Moon, a Manchego, and maybe some cashew cheese. I think it's difficult to deprive yourself of something you love, and I happen to love cheese. I just eat it sparingly. Likewise, we are not strictly gluten-free, just mostly. If we do eat wheat, it is organic and whole grain. At home we cook pasta maybe once a week, usually rice pasta or quinoa pasta, which I think tastes better than wheat pasta anyway, and we all love it when Tom makes his special gluten-free pancakes on the weekends.

By now you probably realize that I'm not too strict. That might be why I'm such a big snacker. During the day you'll usually find me with a handful of almonds toasted with herbs or, my favorite, pumpkin seeds. I also snack on sunflower seeds and, my obsession, *dark chocolate*.

If my husband's first love is football, mine is dark chocolate. I have chocolate every day, even if it's only a bite; and if I have PMS, it's going to be way more than a bite. After lunch, I *always* eat a small dessert, usually something with coconut or, again, dark chocolate, though not often at night, since the caffeine in chocolate can make it hard for me to sleep. The favorite snack in our house is hummus with chopped-up celery, carrots, and cucumbers for dipping. It's usually what we offer to friends when they visit, or bring to a get-together at Benny and Vivi's school. I don't drink alcohol very often, but when I do, I like a glass of red wine, two at the most on special occasions. If I'm on holiday and it's summer, I might have a margarita. I'm not against drinking, but mostly, I don't like the way it makes me feel the next day. Since I have been eating a clean diet and don't drink often, my tolerance for alcohol has become quite low.

I crave different foods depending on whether it's the fall, winter, spring, or summer. Tom and I are members of a local community-supported agriculture (CSA) farm outside of Boston. The members receive a box of whatever vegetables and fruits happen to be in season. In the late fall, for example, we get a ton of squash—which also means we eat lots of it during that time of the year, prepared in a variety of ways.

Nature is intelligent; she tells us what we should eat and *when* we should eat it. When I first moved to Boston and tried to adhere to a mostly vegetarian or vegan diet, I went to bed at night freezing, even with the heat cranked up high. But then I learned to listen to my body. During the colder months, I longed for hot soups and stews, root vegetables, and richer, heavier foods that helped to keep me warm. In the summer, a heavy soup or stew sounds, well, a little heavy. In warm weather, I eat more salads, fruits, and vegetables as well as more raw foods—partly because they are nourishing and cooling and partly because there is such an abundance of them at that time of year. The truth is that locally grown produce just tastes better, because it's fresher. Nothing beats the sweetness of a strawberry in June (even if Tom would disagree with me).

Tom and Vivi with their shades on, Cape Cod, 2014.

Energy—getting more of it—is also the main principle behind my morning workouts. I'm someone who loves using my body, whether I'm doing yoga, skiing (or trying to), surfing, biking, horse-back riding, kickboxing, or dancing, which is one of my all-time fa-vorite activities. I've also had an interest in martial arts. It may be a form of fighting, but I also find it beautiful. I'm a big fan of Bruce Lee. He had a remarkable focus, dedication, and body awareness. Five days a week for almost seven years, I practiced kung fu as well as sword- and stick-fighting in Boston with Yao, an amazing instructor from China. I even practiced during both my pregnancies. The best

Clearing my mind practicing kung fu, 2011.

part was that I could see how much better I was getting every day. Tom used to call me Giselee.

Currently I enjoy doing a variety of different exercises. The most important word in that sentence is *enjoy*. Unless I'm sick or traveling, my morning workout is always part of my routine. I approach exercise the same way I tackle everything else in my life—with 100 percent of my focus and dedication. Whether I'm doing yoga, bands, or dancing, my approach has less to do with wanting to be the best and more with wanting to give my best. I think about it this way: if I take the time to exercise, I want to make the most out of that time. What's the point of doing anything halfway? Whether I'm working out for an hour—which is ideal for me—or twenty or thirty minutes, it's all about presence, dedication, and intensity, no matter what I'm doing.

When I'm in Boston, I usually go to Tom's gym, TB12, twice a week and work out with resistance bands. Fafi and I might do a Pilates or even a dancing class in the Sanctuary. I love exercising outside, especially in Costa Rica. I can be fully integrated and present in nature while also doing good things for my body, brain, and spirit. When I surf, ski, or horseback-ride, I don't ever feel like I'm "working out." For me, exercise is like plugging myself into a high-voltage wall socket. In fact, I get depressed and on edge when I don't exercise, and my vitality diminishes. If we don't take care of our bodies, our bodies won't take care of us. Our bodies are like vehicles. When I exercise and eat well, I'm helping maintain my vehicle so that it works well and doesn't break down. Some people exercise to get a great body. I exercise for sanity and clarity, too. Doing even ten minutes of any type of movement gives me a significant increase of vital energy.

I don't ever want exercise to feel like an obligation. I don't freak out about it or get crazy if I miss a day or two. Compulsive exercise can be as much of a problem as no exercise. If I go surfing, that counts as my workout, though when I get to shore I'll cap my morning off with a few sun salutations if for no other reason than to stretch my muscles that get tight on the surfboard. If Tom and I are out west skiing, and I get in only thirty minutes on the slopes, I might do some band work back at the house. If I'm doing a photo shoot in Brazil, I do yoga in my hotel room, around thirty minutes of hip-openers, planks, bridge poses, and stretches. I go with the flow. Exercise reconnects me to my breath and my body. When I'm working out and being conscious of my breathing, exercise becomes another form of meditation. When I'm done, I feel revitalized.

Except when it's not. Last year, for example, I tore my ACL skiing on the first day of a weeklong vacation with the kids. I was frustrated that for the rest of the trip I had to stay inside with my leg up. For months the most I was allowed to do was walk, and it took me a long time to get back to my daily routines. I now appreciate it more than ever when my body is feeling good, and I understand how important it is to take really good care of it so that I can keep doing what I love for as long as possible. Being immobilized and not being able to exercise regularly was very tough for me and definitely made me a little low. It took patience, dedication, and consistency to recover fully, but today I am so appreciative to have my body back feeling good (except my shoulders still need some work).

There's something very satisfying about focusing on one type of discipline, say, yoga or a martial art, every single day, over a long period of time. Not only do you get to experience your progress, but you're also able to go into the practice with greater depth. For example, when you practice yoga asanas with consistency and focus they can become a gateway to spiritual understanding. Once again, it's about dedication: the more time and attention we give to something, the more we develop. But as with everything, self-awareness goes a long way toward letting you know what works well for your body. What's right for me might not be for you. My choice is to use exercise as a tool for creating inner calm and clarity. What is it for you? A way to find solitude on a long walk or connect with friends at a class? Are you a very high-energy person who needs exercise to ground yourself, or do you tend to be sluggish and need a jolt? Your inspiration and vitality may come from some of the activities I love, or from something else entirely. Maybe you need a variety of activities that complement each other. I don't think it's any accident that Tom's favorite off-season sport is golf—no hitting, no running. Our bodies and the earth are the only two homes we have. How do you want your home to be so you can feel your happiest and best? Are you being loving and kind to yourself, so you can ask for and receive the most from your body and mind? If you haven't given your body the attention and nourishment it needs, it's unlikely that it will give you back what *you* need.

If you're considering making adjustments to your own nutritional regimen, my main recommendation is to avoid sugar and processed foods. Try to eat as much *real* and *local* food as you can. If organic food isn't an option, make sure you wash everything thoroughly. If you want to eliminate sugar or cut back on dairy products, take it slowly. Go step-by-step. See how your body reacts. If you have more energy as a result, you will be motivated to keep going. That's what happened to me. But don't do what I've heard some people have done and take on my "diet" as a challenge. First of all, my diet evolved pretty slowly in the face of circumstances. And second, you won't necessarily react to food the way I do.

Having said all this . . . I. Love. Pizza. Some Saturday nights, when Benny and Vivi have friends over for sleepovers, we have Pizza Night. I try to keep this from being a nutritional disaster by focusing on the ingredients. (The truth is, you can make a lot of your favorite foods—like mac and cheese—into pluses instead of minuses by altering individual ingredients.) A good friend of ours owns a small chain of pizzerias called Desano, which uses high-quality Italian ingredients, and sometimes he sends us batches, which we prepare on those special Saturday nights. The ingredients are organic, and the pizzas themselves have very little cheese, typically burrata (buffalo mozzarella). They are so thin and crunchy it's almost like eating focaccia. Of course, since I'm incapable of wasting food, I usually end up eating everyone's crusts, with real French butter. You won't find me standing in the kitchen at one A.M. devouring ice cream, but once I start eating French butter, I just can't stop. Nothing compares to real French butter on a good piece of bread. We all need a guilty pleasure or two—or three—and real French butter and dark chocolate are mine, along with a tub of popcorn, please, on movie nights with Tom.

By now you might be wondering if our family's nutritional regimen is one that Benny and Vivi actually like given that children are notoriously picky eaters. But the kids have been eating whole foods since they were very young, so they are used to it, and they really like it.

I suppose people tend to like that which is familiar, why people born in England love Earl Grey, Australians love Vegemite, and south Brazilians drink Erva Mate. Our taste buds are primed to love what we know and especially what we knew growing up. Any vegetables my kids can eat raw—cauliflower, cucumbers, carrots, broccoli—they like, along with sliced cucumbers or carrots with hummus, with maybe a sprinkling of Himalayan sea salt on top. Of course, they also love pizza, pasta, and cheeseburgers, which they eat occasionally if we are traveling, but at home we try to keep our diet as healthy as possible.

If my kids have a taste for what they grew up with, that makes the reverse true as well. If you grew up eating cheeseburgers, french fries, and pizza, you'll grow up accustomed to salt, sugar, and fat. If you start eating healthier foods, at first the new taste might not seem as good in comparison because the salt, sugar, fat, and chemicals in processed food are missing. But believe me, you can change your reactions to food and develop an enjoyment of a new diet, and I'm

When children are around good food, and encouraged to make their own, I believe they end up loving quality healthy food. This is Vivi, helping me make green juice in the morning, 2014.

living proof. For me it was a matter of realizing how much better I felt, and the joy of having more vitality. That said, there are a few ways to sneak vegetables into children's diets. My own mom used to chop up vegetables and add them to eggs. Or she would make a chicken-vegetable soup, which I still make when Benny or Vivi are coming down with a cold. You can warm vegetables up in a pan with a little bit of ghee (clarified butter, which I like to use for sautéing), garlic, and sea salt; you can dip them in hummus or nut butter or tahini sauce; you can turn vegetables into smoothies; and you can sneak them into stews, soups, or eggs the way my mom did. I have a friend who makes carrot cookies with organic oatmeal and a whole lot of shredded carrot. Her family loves them. Think about what you like, and use your imagination.

After dinner, I usually like to drink a cup of chamomile tea, and I make cups for the kids, too. Normally I try not to drink anything—whether it's water, tea, or wine—while I'm eating. My mom always taught us girls that it's too hard on the digestive system. Basically I drink whatever I want before dinner, and so do the kids, but usually not during the meal. When dinner is over, I wait at least thirty minutes before I drink liquids. And I'm going to repeat that I'm a big believer in smaller portions. It's really hard on your digestion to take in a lot of food all at once. Think about how you feel the day after Thanksgiving. My philosophy is that if you are still really hungry, you can always have more. I think when we slow down and eat a little more mindfully, it's easier to figure out when the tank is full.

When I was single and childless, I used to go on three- or four-day silent meditation retreats where I would also be on a juice fast. What fascinated me was that after I was done fasting, and began to eat solid food, the first fruit or vegetable I ate exploded in my mouth with flavor. I still like doing the occasional detox because I feel great after it. That said, I would not do a juice detox in the winter, only in the warmer months. Our bodies need as much energy and as many fats as they can get when it's cold out (and believe me, it gets cold in Boston), so I reserve any fasting for the summer months. Sometimes I'll drink only juices. I also drink a lot of coconut water for its nutritional and energetic value (it tastes best when straight from the coconut). It really clears my mind. The first two days of a liquid diet can be challenging, because, well, you're hungry. For me, though, it's all worth it. The detoxing gives me clarity and more energy.

But I don't do fasts as a form of weight control. I maintain my weight through my lifestyle. I eat clean, and I drink a lot of water and tea throughout the day. Whether I'm eating or exercising, it's all about gaining energy and clarity while re-centering myself.

We are what we eat! This won't come as news to most people, but I take it a step further. We are also *how* we eat. It took me years to understand that it isn't just what I put in my mouth that matters—it's also how I am eating—how quickly, but also my emotional state. If I'm anxious or joyful at mealtime, these feelings will be ingested as well. The attitude I like to bring to my meals is appreciation. Appreciation for the miracle of nature, like the little seeds that grew into the vegetables in my salad, or a beautiful tree that has shared its fruit with me. Taking the time to bring a full awareness to meals can deepen our respect for life and nature. When we're more attuned to what we eat, we become even more aware that nature gives us every single element that allows our bodies to flourish.

Have you ever imagined *not* having food? Or, outside of fasting, gone more than one or two days without eating anything? If you have, and someone offered you something to eat, at that moment it would be more valuable to you than anything on earth. For a long time, I was thoughtless about food and eating. I ate automatically and unconsciously. I was hungry—so I fed myself. I ate in a hurry, too, barely chewing my food, especially if I was really hungry. I hardly took a breath between bites. Mealtimes for me were opportunities to catch up on phone calls or take meetings. No wonder I felt sluggish and a little sick after. What had my mom always told us when we were young? To chew our food well, at least twenty times. To this day when our family gets together, my mom is very quiet when she is eating, really taking in every bite.

The way a person eats says a lot about them. What is expressed on the outside is often a reflection of what's on the inside. By now you know meditation has taught me many things, in particular the importance, and magic, of being fully present in any given moment. When we're present, we see, hear, feel, taste, and experience everything more clearly. I don't eat as slowly as my mom does—I'm still working on it—but my intention is to be aware, to try and turn every meal into a form of meditation. Once in a while meals can be a great time to practice awareness by staying silent, focusing on your food, paying attention to your breathing, and watching where your mind wanders as you eat. Life is busy so I don't get to eat every meal this way, but when I do, I feel great!

I also believe it is important to take a moment to ask ourselves what emotions we bring to our food. Do we appreciate what's in front of us? Do we feel grateful? Do we feel guilty about what we're about to eat, or can we eat our meal with pleasure and enjoyment? I realize that emotions surrounding food are complicated and that everyone has their own "thing."

All of this is to say that sitting down for a meal can be a great opportunity to experience presence and gratitude.

It's worth trying out. Sit in silence. Say a short blessing for the food that's in front of you and where it came from. Don't turn it into a contest to see who can eat more slowly, but do take in each bite with an appreciation of all the nutrients you are taking in. See how you feel once you're done. Life is so full and so busy for most of us that we seldom take the time to relax and become centered. But we all need to eat. So why not make mealtime a more mindful experience?

8

Know Thyself

Someone once told me a story about a frog and a well. It's an old story, and maybe you've heard it before but here it goes: Once there was a frog who lived at the bottom of a well. He spent most of his time in the water, and the shadows, and from his vantage point the world seemed familiar and complete and perfect.

I know everything there is to know about everything, the frog thought. *I can see every star and comet and constellation. I can tell the difference between day, night, dusk, and dawn. I know every cloud, every star, and every passing bird.* I know everything there is to know about life.

One day the frog got curious, so he decided to take a leap of faith to check if there was anything beyond the well. When he landed outside, he couldn't believe the whole new world around him. When he looked up at the sky, instead of seeing the small hole-shaped version of reality he'd known his entire life, he saw a huge, ever-changing and completely exhilarating world. There were more stars, comets, clouds, constellations, and birds than he knew existed. There was grass, trees, rocks, and an infinite horizon. He was suddenly aware of the smallness of his own body.

I love this story—it says so much in such a simple way. I think about it a lot because since I left home to begin modeling, I've been on a quest to understand my purpose in life. I was intent on getting out of the well. I wanted to expand myself, and experience as much of life as I possibly could. I've always loved learning new things, and digging deep into subjects that interest me, knowing that with everything I was studying there would always be more to learn. I often feel like the more I learn, the less I know. Who I was at age fourteen isn't who I was at twenty, or who I am today at thirty-eight, or who I'll be a decade from now. But there are some things that never change, like my ongoing process to deepen my understanding of myself, other people, and the world around me. The eighth and last chapter, "Know Thyself," is really the lesson that lies beneath all the others.

What could be more important than knowing ourselves, and continually expanding our self-awareness? Unless we make the effort to understand the many facets of our nature, we won't discover what gives us joy and purpose.

"What you seek is seeking you," Rumi once wrote. My searching has always included books about history, religion, metaphysics, mysticism. I read books on Christianity, Buddhism, and Hinduism. I read the *Bhagavad Gita* and *Siddartha*. I read about the lives of people who inspired me, like Gandhi and Martin Luther King and Krishna Murthy. Once I started, it was hard for me to stop. What was chi? What was dharma? What was numerology? What were chakras? What did the ancient Egyptians know? What about the Mayans? How did Machu Picchu come to exist? When I began meditating and practicing yoga, I entered new worlds and belief systems. And I kept traveling. Sometimes my travels were philosophical. Sometimes they were psychological. Sometimes they had to do with me challenging myself to face down my fears. Sometimes they were geographical.

For example, living in Japan when I was a teenager, and later in New York, and traveling the world on the show circuit, I observed many different cultures, habits, and beliefs, and learned that there really is no "right way to live." In the end, each one of us is responsible for our own life, and for the reality we are helping to create. We each need to decide what kind of human we want to be and where we want to focus our attention. What do we believe? What are values we want to live by? What kind of life do we want to have?

In the course of my reading and travels, I've learned that there are some popular notions that are really quite old. *Know thyself* is inscribed on the Temple of Apollo at Delphi, and may actually have been passed down from the Ancient Egyptians. In this book, I talk about gratitude, but the Bhagavad Gita addressed this same subject six thousand years ago. Meditation and yoga have been around for centuries. I don't pretend to "own" the concepts in these pages. I'm simply doing my best to live them in my own life.

For example, the idea that all people have both male and female energies inside them, and that internal balance is when these two forces are in harmony, comes from Taoism, which dates back to the sixth century BC. In Taoism, the male part is called *yang*, and the female part is called *yin*. The concept that both *yin* and *yang* reside within us probably seems logical to some people but counterintuitive to others. If we identify as a man or a woman, doesn't it make sense that everything a man does is masculine and everything a woman does is feminine?

Not to my way of thinking. Whether you're a man or a woman, each of us has directive, active qualities, *yang*, and receptive, passive qualities, *yin*.

When we are equally comfortable with both strength and sensitivity, action and waiting, listening and speaking, these two extremes within us form balance. That's not to say that attaining balance is easy. Starting at a very young age, we are given messages from parents, siblings, classmates, friends, and the culture telling us how little boys and girls should behave. Boys are meant to be strong, stoic, competitive, and ambitious. Girls are meant to be more receptive, polite, supportive, and empathetic. But how many girls, boys, men, and women fit into one category or another?

I do think that everyone can agree that men and women are not the same. Masculine energy does tend to be assertive and directive, while feminine energy tends to be more receptive and intuitive. Male energy needs to conquer and win, and female energy needs to nurture and protect. *Both* these energies are extraordinary, as long as we work with them consciously, in a balanced way, for the good of *everybody*.

In my experience, the actualization of the male is *power*. The actualization of the female is *love*. By balancing the two and combining power *with* love we can begin to create genuine, positive change in the world and in ourselves. To do that men don't need to become more like women, nor do women need to become more like men. Instead, both genders just need to become more conscious of the masculine and feminine energies that already reside within them. Instead of denying their female energy, men need to embrace it. Instead of

My dad serenading all of us with his guitar—as he did throughout our childhood—in Brazil, 1993.

suppressing their male energy, women should celebrate it. What if you don't identify as male or female, or you love another person of the same sex? Does that mean you're missing out? Hardly. Love is love. If you can embrace your own masculine and feminine energies, and find a partner with that same balance, each of us can find wholeness and then share and learn together."

When I was young I remember being aware of the intricate dance of male/female balance with my parents. On the surface, my dad was much more emotional than my mom. On Sundays, when he brought out his guitar and serenaded us with old gaucho songs, his eyes would fill with tears.

My dad inspired my creativity, my sensitivity, my idealism, and my lifelong sense of purpose—the idea that anything is possible. He encouraged me to dream big, to reject labels, and to be fearless. He still does. He's always been a kid at heart, a little playful, and I'm that way, too. As for the importance of hard work, focus, discipline, and perseverance—all that comes from my mom. From her I learned not to waste, never to throw anything away if it could be repurposed, to be appreciative, and to finish what was on my plate, and to donate anything I no longer needed. She taught me the value of things and how to never take anything for granted and how to be independent. My mom gave all of us a go-and-do-it attitude. That's probably why today I have my own drill and my own toolbox—if something needs to be fixed or hung, I'm the person who'll do it. (At least, I will try before considering calling in a professional.)

Earlier I wrote that as a teenager, I spent a lot of time studying Taoism, the Chinese philosophy that teaches about the *yin* and *yang*. It was both confusing and inspiring. What was the relationship between the sun and the moon, the positive and the negative, the darkness and the light? Were they opposing forces or variations? Over time I came to believe that our masculine and feminine energies are not separate but instead two halves of a perfect whole.

It can be easy to doubt this when we think about how our culture treats boys and girls who don't meet conventional expectations. Even if parents don't come right out and tell their sons and daughters to act a certain way, children pick up nonverbal cues. What is more destructive than to tell a child that he or she shouldn't feel what they're feeling? Does that mean if you're a boy you're not allowed to cry? Does it mean if you're a girl you can't be competitive or ambitious? As a result, many boys grow up believing it's wrong to express their emotions, and many girls feel they should suppress their ambitions.

But why are we here if not to experience the full range of what it is to be human—meaning both our masculine and feminine energies?

Is it any wonder yoga appeals to many women who, remembering how as girls they were told to cover themselves up and quiet their voices, now hold out their arms in warrior pose? Throughout their lives, men and women give and take, lead and follow, direct and receive. If we can't figure out how to yoke together these two energies, I believe we're incomplete, and out of balance, which can lead to all kinds of negative behaviors.

At this time, I believe we're still living in a world where the masculine energy is out of balance. A world where some men continue to abuse power. Men motivated by vanity, ego, and greed. Men willing to sacrifice love, consideration for others, and care for the earth for their own short-term gains. Power without love is a bad combination—and it is unsustainable. We read about this every day in the headlines. Rampant inequality. Cruelty toward the less fortunate. Floating islands of plastic garbage in the ocean. This dominance of masculine energy has disconnected us from the feminine side, and from Mother Earth.

Our survival comes from our earth's natural resources, so wouldn't it be smart for us to use them wisely, so we can continue to utilize and enjoy them for many generations? Using up our natural resources without the awareness that they are finite moves us toward extinction. We need to make sustainable choices, so our earth has time to replenish. Because we haven't been paying attention, the earth is sending us stronger and stronger messages. Tsunamis. Floods. Earthquakes. Droughts. Erupting volcanoes. We forget that when the earth gets sick, we do, too.

Over the years many books have emphasized that the "male" elements are fire and air, while earth and water are "female." As the biggest archetype of the female, the earth is loving, nurturing, sacrificing, and compassionate. She gives and gives, expecting almost nothing back. In return, some men use their power to take advantage of her, as they often do with women. For the sake of dominance. For the sake of power and ego or maybe because of many years of history and repeated behaviors they thought it's their *right*.

Finally, truth about the way many men have misused their power to abuse and exploit women is coming to light. Violence. Pornography. Haters and bullies venting on social media and on comment boards. Our culture is coming face-to-face with its own shadows. But what are shadows anyway? The absence of light. I believe the light contains positive attitudes and actions and as we become more conscious of the changes we need to make, the light will get stronger. It can be easy to want to avoid what is ugly and negative, but the fact that many brave women have publicly addressed their exploitation gives me hope.

As I said earlier, I believe genuine, positive change in the world can only take place when we combine power *with* love. We need them *both*. Power is energy. Power creates. Power is the spark, the surge. Love, by contrast, is a container. It nourishes. It helps a seed grow and thrive.

The mix of the masculine and feminine, or power and love, is a combination that I have been working on synthesizing for years. Sometimes I'm more in tune with my masculine energy. Other times I'm more connected to the feminine. How do I tell if I'm out of balance? When I'm too directive. I find myself pushing to reach my goals at the expense of other people. To reconnect with my feminine side, first I take a few breaths and then I ask myself a few questions. *How am I reaching my goals? How is what I'm doing affecting my children, and my husband, and the rest of my family, and everyone in the community? How will my actions affect the earth, not just today but in the future?* I consistently strive to balance the masculine and feminine energies within me. Without the masculine energy, I won't be able to accomplish my goals. Without the feminine energy, I lack empathy, compassion, consideration, and perspective. I believe that only by finding the balance between the two can we live an empowered and loving life.

I was a tomboy growing up. I still think of myself that way. I was athletic and naturally aggressive. I liked being up at the net spiking a volleyball. Most of my friends at school were boys, too, but not the cool ones—they had no interest in me. I must have been around twelve or thirteen when I decided I'd rather be tough than fragile. It might have been a way of setting myself apart from my twin sister, who was more delicate than I was, more of a "girl's" girl. If a boy told me I couldn't run or climb as well as he could, my response was, *Actually, I can, watch me!* My younger sister Gabi had a big personality and a big mouth to go along with it. She was always speaking her mind to the boys in her class, and if they gave her a hard time I would always stick up for her by saying, *Listen! If you ever talk that way to my sister again, it is over for you. Do you hear me? Over!* I have no idea why they felt intimidated by me. Maybe it was my masculine energy, or maybe it was because I was tall? Growing up, my sisters and I were all very connected to our masculine energy.

That same quality stayed with me when I began modeling.

The fashion world was the perfect setting for me to experience my masculine and feminine energies combined. Modeling is the only industry I know of where women get paid more than men. At work I transformed from being a tomboy who felt more comfortable wearing jeans, T-shirts, and baggy clothes, into channeling whatever look the job required. I was direct, matter-of-fact, and task-oriented, and I became even more so as time went on. But of course the modeling industry is centered on the idealized female form. If my job was to be sexy or flirtatious, I slid into my own feminine energy. Modeling is feminine in that you need to be intuitively aware of the language of your own body. A model needs to be expressive with eyes, hands, and mouth, or the angle of the hips—it's like being an actress in a silent movie.

It was not until I became a mother that I deeply connected to my feminine energy. I felt like a lioness, and that my home had become a cave, and I'd do anything to defend and preserve my cubbies. Giving birth is such an everyday occurrence, but when it happens to you it's magical and profound. If it weren't for women, there would be no future, as they are the only ones who can nourish life into being.

When I met my husband, Tom, in December 2006, on a blind date, I learned quickly that he was a warrior in his sport, pro football. What surprised me, and what I fell most in love with over time was his kindness, gentleness, his sweetness. Tom was and is a solid character. He was as close to his parents and sisters as I am to mine, and I could tell he was very loving and had strong values. It took me no time to realize he would be a good family man. At the time we started dating, both of our careers were in high gear. Like me, Tom was 100 percent dedicated to his job—not that I really understood what football was back then, or what being an NFL quarterback meant. I knew only that Tom loved doing what he did, and was committed to his team, the New England Patriots, and to sustaining his own amazing performance. His goal, he told me, was to play for ten more years and retire, then he wanted to focus on having a family. I was only twenty-six, and to me that sounded like a great plan, as I also felt I still had so much I wanted to accomplish in my career. But life unfolds in unexpected ways—the only constant is change. Two months into our relationship, Tom told me that his ex-girlfriend was pregnant. The very next day the news was everywhere, and I felt my world had been turned upside down. Needless to say, that wasn't an easy time. But it was a time that brought about so much growth. Later that year, little Jack was born, making my heart expand in ways I didn't know was possible.

Jack, my bonus child, has been a huge gift and blessing in my life. In fact, I credit Jack with accelerating Tom's and my growing up in so many ways. The two of us agreed that Jack should have siblings closer to his own age, and not ten years younger. With Jack in our lives, our priorities definitely started to shift. I wanted to be there for Jack and Tom, and do whatever I could to create stability in their lives, and help them to have a close relationship. Tom, especially, needed my support during that time, and whenever I'm in a position to be of help to anyone, especially someone I love, I will be there. The truth is, helping and being supportive of others always makes me feel good. I also know that in order to gain something, very often you have to give something up. We decided to start our own family sooner rather than later. A couple of years later, we were married, I became pregnant, and soon we were busy growing our family between New England and Los Angeles.

Before Tom and I were married, we talked a lot about how we wanted our relationship to develop, and I expressed that I wanted an interdependent relationship, not a codependent one. I see marriage as two people walking side by side, growing individually and together, never giving up the essence of who they are, or their dreams, to please or pacify their partner. I wanted someone who would accept me fully for who I was, someone who inspired and challenged me to be the best version of myself. I wanted to be that same person for my husband. I saw our relationship as a safe port we could both return to for shelter when we needed it, while making sure we both had the freedom to actualize our own dreams.

More than that, I wanted a marriage of equals, one based on love, respect, and trust. I still believe that a marriage of equals—where two people are equally, simultaneously driven in their careers—is possible, but not as easy when the kids are little. Children should come first. I had always dreamed of having a family, and when that dream came true, my children naturally became my priority.

I believe women can do everything—just not all at the same time. We must prioritize. Because the Patriots play in Boston, and Tom's time wasn't his own, I saw it this way: my job as a model had a lot more flexibility than his job. New York may be the center of the fashion industry, but modeling isn't a nine-to-five job, and I didn't need to live in Manhattan to keep doing what I was doing. I also felt I had already accomplished a lot—at least in the fashion industry. I didn't feel the need to keep on proving myself. It hadn't been easy for me to get to the top of the mountain, but after years of hard work, I'd made it. I asked myself, *Do I need one more magazine cover? Do I need one more campaign? Do I need to make one more personal appearance?* Not really! My priority became my family, and experiencing them to the fullest. I wanted to build the best possible relationship with Tom, Jack, and our children. I love nesting and I'm also a peacemaker who likes making everything better, easier, and more harmonious for the people I love. Many women probably know what I'm talking about!

Tom's parents, sisters, and extended family, including nieces and nephews, the day before the epic 2017 Super Bowl, when the Patriots beat the Atlanta Falcons. That's me in the back next to Tom's mom, Galynn.

I never looked back either. Our son, Benny, was born in December 2009, and two months later, when football season was over, Tom, Benny, and I moved out to Los Angeles, where Jack was living, so we could all be with Jack more regularly. But by the early summer, our family was back in Boston in time for training camp.

A new marriage, a new baby, a new life in New England—it was a big transition for me. I didn't know anyone in Boston, and living there made it harder for me to do my work, but I was in love with

Tom and I wanted to make our marriage work. So what I'd worked so hard to achieve, the thing I'd done since the age of fourteen, had to take a backseat. It wasn't a completely smooth transition. My career had been centered on just one person's needs: mine. I could come and go, work and travel here and there, and do what *I* wanted to do. That chapter of my life was replaced by the needs of a growing family. With the arrival of Benny and Vivi, I found out quickly that being a mother was a lot more work than modeling. Any mother with little kids knows that the job is consuming. Tom's schedule during football season is so demanding that I take on most of the family responsibilities.

I think of this stage of my life as The Valley. Not because it is in any way negative, but because once you've been on top of the mountain, there's nowhere else to go but back down. On top of a mountain, it's always sunny and bright and you get a big view. In contrast, life in a valley is quieter and more contained. The Valley gives me the opportunity to understand a different side of myself, and to devote myself to being the best wife and best mother I can be, all while I get to experience the love of my children.

I was fortunate, though. Unlike many full-time mothers, I'd had the opportunity to start working at a very young age, and my many years of hard work had given me financial freedom. I still have the opportunity to travel for contract work, and any other free time I have dedicated to the causes that matter to me. Those jobs and trips are like quick visits back to the mountaintop—whether I was walking the runway at the Rio Olympics or giving a speech about the environment before the United Nations. But I turn down most modeling jobs. Either Tom has a big game, or Benny has a play at school, or maybe Jack will be with us for the weekend, or Vivi has a bad cough. For whatever the reason, the scheduling doesn't always work, and my family comes first.

When the kids were very young, there were times when I felt overwhelmed or conflicted, sometimes a little depressed, though I tried my best to be strong. I felt the massive new responsibility of motherhood. I wanted to do my best, and to do it right. The thing is, I was an inexperienced mom, in on-the-job training, plus I sometimes felt torn, since I knew I had so much more I wanted to create in the world. Tom helped out as much as possible, but during the season, he's gone by six in the morning and I usually don't see him until dinner. Thank God my mom stayed for a month after Benny was born. Without my mom, Fafi, and Mayra, my friend and doula, who, after a lot of convincing, became our babysitter for a while, I don't think I could have managed as well as I did.

At the same time, I'd been connected my whole life to my own masculine energy. *Accomplish, accomplish, accomplish! Go, go, go!* When I was pregnant with Benny, I decided to learn how to fly a helicopter. (Talk about embracing my masculine energy.) I found a local pilot named Stu, and for the next three months took an intensive course in navigation, weather patterns, stratus clouds, cumulus clouds, and the effects of condensation on flying. I learned how to fly at night and in bad weather, how to land a helicopter in a confined area and talk with the air-traffic controllers in the tower. I put in the sixty hours needed to get certified as a private helicopter pilot, though I stopped short of getting my license, since Tom and I both felt it was too dangerous for me to do the final test, which involved making an emergency landing with no throttle. Still, it was fun going through the whole process. I was flying an R44 helicopter—"the bird," as Stu and I called it—a few days before Benny was born!

Benny and I feeling proud and strong after completing our sixty hours of helicopter training in 2009. Benny was born about a month later.

The Valley also reminds me of the importance of the feminine element in the life of any family. If you're a man or a woman who works outside the home, you lead two very different lives. The first life, your outside life, takes place out in the world. It centers on drive and achievement and making a living to support your family. The second life is your *inside* life. This one is focused on taking care of the house and the children; keeping the calendar; staying on top of a million details like babysitters, school stuff, doctor's appointments, and social obligations; and making sure everyone is doing okay and everything is running smoothly. Most men are focused on their outside lives and many women are, too. But for anyone to succeed and thrive in their *outside* life, they need to have a strong, stable *inside* life.

That's why, if I ever hear someone saying, "She's just a mom," it makes me angry. Being "just a mom" is the foundation of *everything.* Being "just a mom" ensures that our children have the foundation and support they need to succeed not just at work but at life. Millions of "just moms" are busy raising future men and women who will some-day influence the world in either positive or negative ways. Our culture likes to treat the daily multitasking that women perform as something to be expected. They're not. There are a lot of mothers out there who make everything possible and everything happen, and I think they're amazing.

As time went on, I became more and more aware that I was out of balance. With two small children, a household to oversee, and a husband working all day and sometimes out of town for away games, I realized I wasn't in a very healthy place. That's when I started making small changes. Instead of staying by myself at home caring for the children, I would invite a friend over for tea. Then another friend for a walk. When I went back to work, I took Benny and Vivi along with me so I could breast-feed. It was an intense period. I was getting almost no sleep at night and working all day. I felt like a zombie. One time I remember breast-feeding Benny on a long plane trip to Brazil and feeling like the worst mother in the world, even though I knew I'd feel even worse if I'd left him at home. Still, going back to work after having children felt like I was going on vacation! Slowly I began to regain my own balance of masculine and feminine energies. I was also able to see how this same balance was forming in my *own* children.

Jack and Benny are already connected to their more "sensitive," intuitive sides. At five, Vivi is already very strong and her style is my-way-or-the-highway! She's single-minded and driven to reach her goals. At the same time, she is extremely loving, and extremely smart. She has her father wrapped around her finger, and she knows it, too. She is always so happy and sunny and joyful that we all say Vivi is skipping through life. Benny, who's eight, loves music and art and singing and building with LEGOs. He loves animals and the earth so one night after I had just returned from a trip to the Amazon, we were talking about what each of us could do to help protect life on earth. He asked me what he could do. I suggested that instead of receiving gifts for his birthday, he could ask his friends to use the money and make donations to help to protect his favorite animals. So for the past two years on his birthday, his friends made donations to help him save the elephants and the whales. He has a lot of empathy, and also likes spending time alone dreaming, in the same way I did at his age. Of the three, Jack, the oldest, is the most responsible and also has a healthy balance of masculine and feminine energies. He's extremely dedicated, loves playing soccer, and once told his dad that someday he wants to go to Michigan, Tom's alma mater. (Of course Tom beamed.) Like his father, he is also kind, sensitive, and generous. I feel so lucky I get to have them all in my life. I love them so much!

My role, as I see it, is to be their guardian, and to allow each one to realize his or her innate strengths and talents. I also try to set an example with my own masculine and feminine energies, so they can see I'm both strong *and* nurturing.

Now that the kids are older and in school, I know that soon I'll be ready to begin climbing another mountain. (I learned I'm good at climbing mountains!) I've never lived in The Valley for this long, but

I wouldn't give back the time I spent there for anything. My children have given me a greater sense of purpose and motivation. Before they were born, I was passionate about ecological and environmental causes. But now I bring a hundred times more dedication, drive, and urgency to that same work. Having children made it even more important to me to help make the world a better place.

Recently Tom and I revisited the conversation we had when we first got married, the one where he told me he would play for ten more years, then retire. But I acknowledge that it's been better for both of us to think of that conversation as a map, not as the destination. Today Tom is playing better than he ever has, and he still loves what he's doing. I have never met anyone in my whole life who loves anything as much as my husband loves playing football! I am in awe of the commitment, focus, and tireless dedication he puts into being the best at what he does. At the same time, we both know that an athlete's career is limited. I worry about his physical health. Like any wife, I am scared for him, and for our family, too, because football is such a physical sport. But I am not going to tell him to stop doing what he loves. His dedication and discipline and commitment to being the best at what he does are some of the reasons I love him. Tom will retire when he feels it's time. The decision has to come from him. In the end, if Tom is happy, we are *all* happy.

One of the things about being a woman, a wife, and a mother is that I'm always looking out for what is best not just for me, or for Tom, but for everybody in our family. What is the best way to support and fulfill *everybody's* needs as we move forward? In that sense, women have a lot in common with the earth.

What matters most to me right now—it's my number-one

priority, in fact—is that Benny, Vivi, and Jack grow up together in a stable environment. That they can grow and feel part of a community and make good lasting friendships. I want them all to feel safe and loved, and to know they can always count on one another, that they have a strong, solid foundation in our family and our community, and that Tom and I will always be there for them, no matter what.

Wherever the two of us end up living, *home* isn't a literal place or structure, with paint or bricks or windows or rugs. Home to me is about memories, emotions, and amazing moments. The apartments and houses I've lived in are settings for love, good times, all of us spending time togther and laughing over a meal. *Home* for me is a place inside me. It's wherever my family is.

Sometimes I tell people that my husband and I love each other so much we got married twice. Tom and I both come from strong, solid, very close-knit Roman Catholic families—especially my mom's family (she even had a sister who was a nun). Our parents have been married for decades. It mattered a lot to our families that Tom and I had a traditional marriage ceremony, in a church, and of course we both wanted to honor their wishes.

Our first ceremony took place on February 26, 2009, when we said our vows inside Saint Monica's Catholic Church in Santa Monica, California. Aside from Tom, me, and our pastor Lloyd, who married us, the only attendees were our parents and Jack, who was two at the time and the ring bearer. A couple of our good friends were there, too; one was in charge of taking photographs, though during the ceremony he got so emotional that most of the pictures ended up out of focus. After the ceremony, we all drove back to our house for salad, cake, and steaks that Tom grilled. That was our wedding reception.

Growing up, I don't remember having any fairy-tale fantasies about getting married. I never pictured myself in a big white dress, for example, or surrounded by bridesmaids. No, I imagined my marriage being more unconventional than that. If I got married, it would be in nature, which is my *real* church, and the ceremony would be fun, beautiful, and informal. I would go barefoot. I would say my vows right as the sun was going down. The first time I visited Costa Rica, I fell in love with its raw nature and thought, *I hope I can live here someday.*

Costa Rica reminded me so much of Brazil—the weather, the humidity, the same kind, loving, simple people. There are monkeys and birds in the trees, dolphins and pelicans in the ocean, and millions of

My first trip to Costa Rica, 1998, when I fell head over heels in love with the country. I was eighteen.

butterflies. The landscape is damp and alive, as if it's breathing in and out. In my twenties, when I began making more money, I bought a plot of land in a remote section of the country and began having a house built. I thought it would be the perfect setting for a wedding.

In the weeks before our church ceremony, Tom and I spent a lot of time talking about what we wanted in our relationship. As I said earlier, I expressed to Tom that the last thing I wanted from our marriage was codependence. When you feel you need to save the other person. When you spend the whole time worrying about his needs to the point that they subsume or become your own. When you feel the need to rescue him or fix him. What could be more dangerous than being in a relationship where your partner can't breathe without you, or when a partner needs you to make him whole, or when he's responsible for filling in parts of yourself you lack, and you lose yourself and your own identity? No, our marriage not only had to be based on love, respect, and honesty; it had to be *interdependent*—where two strong people love each other but never to the point of sacrificing their own happiness or values. To me, marriage, or any relationship, comes down to two people walking side by side through life, learning alone and together, and sharing what they've learned with each other as they keep growing and expanding.

I wasn't Tom; Tom wasn't me. We loved each other, but we weren't the same person. For the rest of our lives, we would both be changing. So many marriages I know of end when one partner accuses the other of just that, *changing*. But what are we supposed to do if not keep changing throughout our lives? Trees lose their leaves in the fall, sleep in the winter, bud in the spring, and come alive in the summer. The sun comes out, followed by rain, or snow, or clouds, or more sun. People are similar! As I found out when I was living in The Valley, there is a natural rhythm to everything, a time to contract and a time to expand, a rhythm that can repeat many times over a single lifetime.

Just as I'd once imagined, Tom's and my wedding ceremony in Costa Rica was, as I hoped, fun, beautiful, and informal—more spiritual than religious.

I've known a lot of brides who get stressed out in the weeks before their weddings, worrying about the photographer, or the food, or the bartender, or which bridesmaid was wearing what dress. I didn't want to think about those things. What I *did* think about in the weeks before the ceremony was what I'd admired in other marriages I knew. Similar to the balance of masculine and female energies inside all of us, the ideal marriage is a dance in which both partners take turns giving and taking, leading and following, directing and receiving, for

Costa Rica wedding.

the rest of their lives. I believe that a woman who has those two energies in balance will attract a partner with that same balance. Remember, ideally each one of us is both powerful *and* loving. Strong *and* compassionate.

I've always loved poetry, and a month before our wedding in Costa Rica, I found a poem that really spoke to me. It's from Kahlil Gibran's *The Prophet*, and it was written almost a hundred years ago.

You were born together, and together you shall be forevermore
You shall be together when the white wings of death scatter
 your days
Ay, you shall be together even in the silent memory of God
But let there be spaces in your togetherness
And let the winds of the heavens dance between you
Love one another, but make not a bond of love
Let it rather be a moving sea between the shores of your souls
Fill each other's cup but drink not from one cup
Give one another of your bread but eat not from the same loaf
Sing and dance together and be joyous, but let each one of you
 be alone
Even as the strings of a lute are alone though they quiver with the
 same music
Give your hearts, but not into each other's keeping
For only the hand of Life can contain your hearts
And stand together yet not too near together
For the pillars of the temple stand apart
And the oak tree and the cypress grow not in each other's shadow

The poem reminded me that two people in love *can* attain both interdependence and balance. With that balance, you each become a pillar strong enough to sustain love while living side by side. One partner doesn't need to lean on, or crash into, or merge with the other. A strong pillar stands straight on its own. It's perfect just by being itself, and from that place it chooses to share and to stand with another.

Our wedding took place at sunset on a warm day in early April. Before the ceremony, my sister Fafi helped me do my hair. I wore waterproof mascara since I knew I was going to cry—because I always cry!—and it wouldn't have been a pretty sight having raccoon eyes at my own wedding. Around forty people gathered in our open living room: Tom's and my entire extended family—including nieces—and three good friends apiece. On a nearby table strewn with candles and assorted crystals sat two bowls, one containing honey and the other rice. The honey, it is said, would sweeten our future, and the rice anticipates prosperity. Jack was two, and still our ring bearer! I wore a simple white slip dress. My feet were bare. The ceremony was brief, and the last words anyone heard were:

For the pillars of the temple stand apart
And the oak tree and the cypress grow not in each other's shadow

There was no formal wedding reception afterward. It was more like a free-for-all, a joyful, relaxed party, just the way I'd always imagined it would be. People ate Mexican food and drank margaritas. They sat or stood in the kitchen, or on the lawn, or by the side of the pool. My sister Pati and Tom's sister Julie each read a beautiful poem, and everyone had a slice of the chocolate wedding cake. Tom had made playlists—his had songs by Ray LaMontagne, Amos Lee, James Taylor, and others—and at some point my friend Nino, whom I've known since my earliest days in New York and who's like a brother to me, plugged in his iPod. The kids went swimming in the pool, while guests danced around in their bathing suits. I remember drinking two margaritas, and after two margaritas you don't remember or care about very much.

But I do remember looking for, and finding, Tom, and though I can't remember who led and who followed—does it matter?—we started to dance. We are still dancing, and growing through the ups and downs of life.

So here's a thought experiment: Imagine what would happen if each one of us knew ourselves as fully and deeply as possible. And that we led each day of our lives consciously and compassionately, without projecting our emotions onto others, or allowing our egos to

Tom and I dancing at our wedding reception in Costa Rica, 2009.

distort reality. If everyone did whatever work was necessary to get to know themselves better, and took responsibility for being the best self he or she could be, I believe the world would be a different place, a better place.

So where do you even begin? How can you unlock the door, or to put it another way, how can you jump outside the well? There is *no* best way. There's *your* way. There are millions of different ways for us to get to know ourselves, and your method of diving deep is unique to you. Remember, we are all here to learn lessons. In my experience we get into trouble only when we follow others, instead of following our inner voice and own individual path—of course, always coming from love while respecting others. As I always remind my children, we must treat others as we would like to be treated.

That's why I encourage you to travel—in your head, in your heart, in your beliefs. You could begin by paying close attention to your thoughts, words, and actions. Or by starting a meditation practice. Or by asking yourself questions. Reading books. Getting inspired by people whose lives you admire. Seeking out others who are wise and compassionate from whom you can learn new things. Investigating ancient traditions and belief systems. If you're inclined that way, exploring mythology, or mysticism. Most of all, try to avoid being judgmental, of yourself and other people—and especially being righteous. The world is filled with people who claim that their way of doing things, or their belief system, is right, and others' is wrong. Well, how do we even know what's right and what's wrong?

In the end, we all have choice. Are we going to believe what other people say is true, or are we going to choose to search in ourselves to find our truth?

Put another way, if you're inside the well, jump! I know—it takes courage. You don't know what's out there. That frog certainly didn't. But once you take the leap, you'll be exposed to more stars and sky than you ever knew existed. You'll land someplace new, and maybe even disorienting, a place that expands and deepens your understanding of yourself, the world, your place in that world, and even doorways to other worlds. Why not explore and go through them, too? The universe is infinite and our understanding of it is so small.

Wherever you choose to go, I wish you a safe, exciting journey, and that you may always be connected and guided by love.

ACKNOWLEDGMENTS

When I was a teenager, I wrote in my diary every day, sometimes gluing photos I liked to the pages. At the beginning of every year I would start a fresh one. My diaries were a good way for me to recap my days and take note of what really mattered to me. At age seventeen, when my work became more demanding, I wrote less and less until one day I just stopped. In many ways, writing this book brought me back to those early times. It has become an extension of my diary writing, but on a larger scale. It's been an incredible process—mostly because by asking myself, *What have you learned over the past thirty-eight years?* I've been able to see my own life outside of myself and understand myself better. My dad was right when he told me that if you ever feel unclear about anything, write it down and it will all start to make sense.

Along with giving me the opportunity to look back on my life from the outside in, writing this book has been scary but also liberating. Like most people, I'm not comfortable showing my vulnerabilities to anyone outside my family. But I've experienced a feeling of freedom taking down my walls and allowing who I really am to shine through. Why do I even need these walls anymore?

One lesson of this book is that the quality of our lives depends on the quality of our relationships. In that regard I've been blessed by the people who surrounded me when I first decided to write a book. First, I'm very grateful to my collaborator, Peter Smith. I call Peter "my therapist," and I'm only half joking! Thank you, Peter, for being a fantastic listener and sounding board, and an overall awesome person to spend time with. Thank you to my editor, Caroline Sutton, who asked the right questions, and who understood early on what this book was about and what *I* was about. I'm also grateful to my literary agent, Jim Levine, for his kindness and support through this process, and for helping me place this book with Avery. And my friend Tal, who offered great advice on this project. It mattered a lot to me to work with people who I felt understood me—and my team was with me every step of the way. Thank you, Anne, for being by my side for twenty years, and always being game for a new adventure.

Of course I'm forever grateful to my family, because without them I wouldn't be who I am. Thank you to my parents for giving me life; for a safe, loving home to grow up in with amazing sisters; for always trusting, loving, and supporting me; and for being incredible teachers. Thank you to my sisters for always telling me the truth, even when I don't want to hear it, and for being the best friends anyone could ever have, for always being by my side, for being so supportive of my new adventures, and for providing an awesome support system. I couldn't do what I do without all of you!

To my children—thank you for your love and for always inspiring me to be a better person and to work to make the world a better place. To my husband, Tom—thank you for being a wonderful teacher, a great partner, and a wonderful supporter of my dreams. You have allowed me to expand in ways I couldn't imagine. To all my friends—thank you for your continuing love and support. I also want to thank everyone who has ever crossed my path in the past thirty-eight years, in ways large or small, who has affected the direction of my life. I'm grateful and honored that you've been a part of my journey so far. Finally, thank you to all my beautiful puppies—especially Vida, my guardian angel.